WRITE!

Foundations and Models for Proficiency

CURRICULUM ASSOCIATES®, Inc.

FOR THE STUDENT

WRITE! gives you the tools to be a better writer. You'll enjoy writing more, and you may even improve your writing scores!

FOUNDATIONS

In Part I, you'll think about and practice grammar, usage, and mechanics skills. You'll also study models of various kinds of writing, and you'll do some writing of your own!

MODELS

In Part II, you'll use what you've learned in Part I as you study models of several different forms of writing. For each form of writing, you will

- see prompts and writing models.
- read partner and teacher comments on writing.
- correct errors in writing models.
- learn about rubrics, which are used to score writing.
- score some writing models on your own.
- do your own writing, with tips for help.
- work with a partner to score and improve your writing.
- make connections between writing and other parts of your life.

So, let's start to *WRITE!*

Acknowledgments

Product Development

Dale Lyle *Project Editor*

Joan Krensky *Project Editor*

Joan Talmadge *Project Editor*

Helen Byers *Writer*

J. A. Senn *Content Reviewer*

Design and Production

Susan Hawk *Designer/Illustrator*

Yvonne Cronin *Typesetter*

Photo/Illustration Credits

Page 4 Masters/Corel

Pages 6, 8, 20, 26, 34, 40, 42 ClipArt Explosion

Pages 10, 12, 14, 16, 22, 24, 28, 30, 36, 38, 46, 50, 54, 56, 58, 60, 135 Clipart.com

Page 18 Redwood National Park

Pages 32, 137 Library of Congress

Page 44 U.S. Environmental Protection Agency, Karen Holland

Pages 48, 52 National Park Service

Page 140 photos.com

Page 144 Chameleon Publishing

ISBN 0-7609-2465-1

©2004—Curriculum Associates, Inc.
North Billerica, MA 01862

TABLE OF CONTENTS

LESSON 1

THINK ABOUT

Well-chosen **nouns** can add clarity, richness, and appeal to your writing.

A **noun** is a word that names a person, place, thing, or idea.

- A **concrete noun** names a person, place, or thing that can be seen or touched.

  These words are **concrete nouns**: *ballerina, anthropologist, carpenter, arrow, vineyard, Italy, calculator, pamphlet, suspenders, orangutan.*

- An **abstract noun** names an idea, which cannot be seen or touched.

  These words are **abstract nouns**: *July, ancestry, opinion, withdrawal, urgency, wetness, taste, din, aggression, clarity, foolishness, vigilance.*

These **concrete nouns** name **people**: *neighbor, trooper, plumber, pilot, judge, infant, aunt, Daphne, Mrs. Sanchez, Dr. Lewis.*

These **concrete nouns** name **places**: *beach, basement, courtyard, theater, forest, Avanzo's Bakery, North Dakota, Crater Lake, Mauna Loa, Antarctica.*

These **concrete nouns** name **things**: *anchor, broom, magnet, pendant, keyboard, gravestone, cauliflower, tarantula, Pluto, food.*

These **abstract nouns** name **ideas**: *bounty, universe, purpose, time, depth, fragrance, observation, acceptance, ferocity, selfishness.*

STUDY A MODEL

Read the paragraph from a book on art history.

    Late in the nineteenth century, the Impressionist painters shared an idea. Each of these artists saw extraordinary beauty in the ordinary. Train stations, bridges, farms, and fields became their subjects. Light was their inspiration. They painted outside to capture visual truth. The technique of many Impressionist painters was to paint pure colors in dots and dashes on the canvas. Monet, Degas, and Renoir were masterful with this form.

Concrete nouns are red, and abstract nouns are blue.

In the first and second sentences, the words *painters* and *artists* are concrete nouns. They name types of people, who can be seen.

Notice that the words *beauty, ordinary, subjects,* **and** *inspiration* are abstract nouns. They name ideas, which cannot be seen or touched.

The words *Monet, Degas,* and *Renoir* are concrete proper nouns, naming specific people.

PRACTICE

A *Label each underlined noun C for concrete or A for abstract.*

1. that <u>philosopher</u>
2. an <u>argument</u>
3. an <u>antique</u>
4. a <u>pharaoh</u>
5. many <u>pleasures</u>
6. a <u>rainbow</u>
7. the <u>Mitchell Laboratory</u>
8. his <u>attitude</u>
9. the <u>freeway</u>
10. their <u>laughter</u>

B *Read the sentences. Write the 8 concrete nouns and the 8 abstract nouns.*

1. The elephants had to leave the fragile environment.
2. Will the three jugglers perform in the main tent?
3. A poorly packed backpack can actually cause injury.
4. That old ceramic pitcher may be considered art.
5. His specialty was designing huge mobiles.
6. This technique is a classic.
7. For safety, we hired an experienced guide.
8. How is Julienne doing with the experiment?

C *Read the paragraph. Write the 11 concrete nouns and the 11 abstract nouns. One concrete noun is used more than once.*

  Although it is difficult to imagine, there was a time when many young children had full-time jobs. Though their wages were low, they needed to support their families. Some youngsters worked for twelve hours a day in dirty mines. Other children sold papers, worked on farms, or labored in mills. The working conditions were often dangerous. Many young workers suffered ill health, and some even died as a result of their employment. The laws eventually corrected the wrongs that these children suffered. Now, if young people work, it is highly regulated.

A **concrete noun** names a person, place, or thing that can be seen or touched.
An **abstract noun** names an idea, which cannot be seen or touched.

WRITE

Write a paragraph describing yourself to someone who has never met you. Include interesting concrete and abstract nouns in your writing.

Writing Tip

Two other kinds of nouns are **compound nouns** and **collective nouns**.

Compound nouns are made up of more than one word. Some have hyphens, and others do not.

- My *sister-in-law* does a *broadcast* every *evening*.

Collective nouns name a group of persons or things.

- The *audience* applauded wildly for our *class*.

NOUN SUFFIXES

THINK ABOUT

Some nouns have special endings called **noun suffixes**.

Common Noun Suffixes

-ance	-cide	-ent	-ian	-ist	-or
-ant	-dom	-er	-ice	-ity	-ship
-ary	-ee	-ery	-ion	-ment	-ster
-ation	-ence	-hood	-ism	-ness	-ure

The suffixes *-ation* and *-ion* mean "the act of, the result of." *declaration, preparation, investigation, motivation*

The suffix *-ee* means "one that receives or benefits from a specific action." *trainee, refugee*

The suffixes *-er* and *-or* mean "one who does something." *inventor, reader*

The suffix *-hood* means "group of, state of being." *neighborhood, childhood, brotherhood*

The suffix *-ship* means "quality of, ability or skill." *friendship, township*

You can add a noun suffix to a noun to form a noun with a different meaning.

Noun		Noun Suffix		Noun
state	+	hood	=	statehood
author	+	ship	=	authorship

You can also add a noun suffix to a verb to form a noun.

Verb		Noun Suffix		Noun
instruct	+	ion	=	instruction
inform	+	ation	=	information
sing	+	er	=	singer
develop	+	ment	=	development

And you can add a noun suffix to an adjective to form a noun.

Adjective		Noun Suffix		Noun
curious	+	ity	=	curiosity
young	+	ster	=	youngster

Notice that the spelling of some words changes when a noun suffix is added.

inspire + ation = inspiration (the *e* is dropped)
adverse + ity = adversity (the *e* is dropped)
silly + ness = silliness (the *y* is changed to *i*)

STUDY A MODEL

Read the entry Ramón wrote in his travel journal.

As we approached the city, I was struck with **amazement**. I had no **familiarity** with this part of my country. I had never expected the spectacular **architecture** of the buildings. Headlights and neon glimmered through the fog, making the city seem like a comic-book **kingdom**. Though the air was hot and thick outside, I felt no **humidity** in the **enclosure** of the car. Thankfully the **driver** was my Aunt Carmen, and she was skilled at **navigation**. At her **invitation**, I relaxed. I came to the **conclusion** that being a **tourist** was no boring **activity**!

Nouns with suffixes are red.

 Notice that the noun *amazement* is formed by adding the noun suffix *-ment* to the verb *amaze*.

 The noun *humidity* is the adjective *humid* with the noun suffix *-ity* added.

 Notice that the final *e* in the verb *invite* is dropped before adding the noun suffix *-ation*.

PRACTICE

A *Read each phrase. Write the noun and then underline the noun suffix.*

1. a first-rate accomplishment
2. displeasure was evident
3. one terrific trucker
4. independence was won
5. with touching sincerity
6. a surprised declaration
7. the strangest reaction
8. their loving relationship
9. showed true heroism
10. his rare appearance
11. dependents are invited
12. a visiting dignitary
13. an impolite youngster
14. the finest pianist

B *Read each sentence. Use the noun suffix in parentheses to form a noun from the underlined verb or adjective.*

1. The <u>fierce</u> of her voice surprised us. (ness)
2. Justin's <u>intelligent</u> was finally rewarded. (ence)
3. I appreciated the <u>wise</u> of her advice. (dom)
4. The forecaster predicted the storm's <u>severe</u>. (ity)
5. Imelda has been an <u>employ</u> here for years. (ee)
6. The Olsens' <u>create</u> is truly unusual. (ion)
7. The instructor emphasized the <u>important</u> of listening. (ance)
8. Our <u>friend</u> was strengthened by the experience. (ship)

C *Read the paragraph. Use a noun suffix to create a noun from each of the 10 underlined words. Each noun should make sense in the sentence.*

The moment of our <u>depart</u> was being determined by the weather. As we sat in the harbor, our <u>navigate</u> glanced at the compass and then at his watch. There was a new <u>develop</u>. Our arrival at our chosen spot for a <u>vacate</u> would be delayed. We felt both <u>annoy</u> and <u>anticipate</u>. We longed for the <u>move</u> and the <u>free</u> of the open sea. We tried to stifle our <u>frustrate</u>. Our <u>friend</u> was being tested. But we were set to go!

Some nouns end with a **noun suffix,** such as *-ee, -hood, -ion,* or *-ship.*

WRITE

Write a travel guide entry that describes a place you have been to or have read about. Use nouns to bring the sights alive for the reader. Include some nouns that have noun suffixes. Be sure to spell them correctly.

Writing Tip

You can also add **suffixes to nouns** to form **adjectives.**

Nouns		Suffixes		Adjectives
joy	+	ous	=	joyous
mercy	+	ful	=	merciful (the y is changed to i)
universe	+	al	=	universal (the e is dropped)
king	+	ly	=	kingly

POSSESSIVE NOUNS

THINK ABOUT

A noun changes form to show possession, ownership, or relationship. A **possessive noun** makes clear who or what owns something.

Add an apostrophe and an *s* ('s) to a singular noun to make it possessive.

Singular Nouns	Possessive Nouns
the uniform of a *worker*	a *worker's* uniform
the color of the *sky*	the *sky's* color
the effect of the *law*	the *law's* effect
an opera by *Verdi*	*Verdi's* opera
the bag belonging to *Jo*	*Jo's* bag

Add an apostrophe and an *s* even if the singular noun ends in *s*.

Singular Nouns	Possessive Nouns
a tip for the *waitress*	the *waitress's* tip
the bloom of a *lotus*	a *lotus's* bloom
the shirt belonging to *Chris*	*Chris's* shirt

Add only an apostrophe (') to a plural noun that ends in *s* to make it possessive.

Plural Nouns	Possessive Nouns
the wings of the *planes*	the *planes'* wings
the appearance of the *girls*	the *girls'* appearance
a performance by the *singers*	the *singers'* performance
the house of the *Hugheses*	the *Hugheses'* house
the plans of the *friends*	the *friends'* plans

Add an apostrophe and an *s* ('s) to a plural noun that does not end in *s*.

Plural Nouns	Possessive Nouns
the ideas of the *women*	the *women's* ideas
the wishes of the *people*	the *people's* wishes
the feet of both *mice*	both *mice's* feet
the prints of three *deer*	three *deer's* prints
the antics of four *sheep*	four *sheep's* antics
the yokes of the *oxen*	the *oxen's* yokes

STUDY A MODEL

Read the passage from a family memoir.

In those days, Blue Bluff's finest street followed the cliff's edge. Our dilapidated mansion dominated the street. That summer, our grandparents' rockers creaked on the paint-chipped verandah. The floorboards' squeaks added to the sound. Meanwhile the twins' ongoing cries of glee shattered the serenity of every evening's dusk. Augustus's trike always lay toppled in the forsythia. Mice's nests filled the pantry! Irish setters' collars turned up constantly in flowerpots and other unlikely places. It was chaos, but we were too happy to care.

> Singular possessive nouns are red, and plural possessive nouns are blue.

Notice that *Blue Bluff's* and *cliff's* are both singular possessive nouns. They are formed by adding *'s*.

Grandparents' and *floorboards'* are both plural possessive nouns formed by adding only an apostrophe.

The word *Mice's* is also a plural possessive noun. It is formed by adding *'s*.

Irish setters' is a plural possessive compound noun. It is formed by adding an apostrophe (') to the second word.

PRACTICE

A *Rewrite each phrase using a possessive noun.*

1. a painting by Michelangelo
2. the schedule for the pilots
3. the garden of the Johnsons
4. the supplies of the children
5. the edge of the ocean
6. the preference of the politicians
7. the chair belonging to the boss

B *Read each sentence. Write the singular possessive or the plural possessive form of the underlined noun.*

1. I was always fascinated by <u>Grandma</u> stories.
2. In the 1930s, she lived in her two <u>cousins</u> house.
3. Then <u>people</u> lives were less complicated.
4. A <u>homemaker</u> kitchen was not as well equipped as it is today.
5. A <u>family</u> food was stored in an icebox.
6. All <u>ladies</u> hairstyles were closely cropped and curled.
7. The <u>childrens</u> chores were hard work.
8. The <u>nation</u> classrooms were more formal than those of today.

C *Read the paragraph. Rewrite it, correcting the 9 nouns that are written incorrectly.*

What an evening we had at the seasons opening performance! Streamers hung from the auditoriums high ceiling. The musicians instruments were gleaming. All shuffling hushed as the conductors baton tapped. The singers voices rose as the instruments played. At the end of the performance, an eruption of clapping expressed the people appreciation. The next day, rave reviews in the city two newspapers delighted both choir and orchestra. Two critics articles noted that the many trumpets "golden sounds" were the highlight of the evening.

A **possessive noun** shows who or what owns something. To form a possessive: add 's to a singular noun; add ' to a plural noun that ends in s; add 's to a plural noun that does not end in s.

WRITE

Write a passage about a family event you will always remember. Include some possessive nouns and be sure to write them correctly.

Writing Tip

Pronouns also show **possession**: *my, your, his, her, its, our, their; mine, yours, his, hers, its, ours, theirs.*

Where is *your* friend?

Doug loaned Haley *his* jacket.

The first two seats are *ours.*

Which kitten is *yours?*

SUBJECT AND OBJECT PRONOUNS

THINK ABOUT

To avoid repetition in your writing, use **personal pronouns** to take the place of some nouns. The nouns replaced are called *antecedents*. The pronouns may be **subject pronouns** or **object pronouns**, depending on their use.

Subject Pronouns: *I, we, you, he, she, it they*

Use a **subject pronoun** to take the place of a noun that is used as a subject.

> *Dan* called last night. *He* will call again tonight.
> *Emma* practiced daily, and *she* made the team.

When a subject pronoun is part of a **compound subject**, make sure the pronoun is in the correct **form** and in the correct **order**.

> *He* does homework. *I* do homework.
> *He and I* do homework. (not *he and me* or *me and him* or *I and he*)

Use a **subject pronoun** to take the place of a noun that follows a **linking verb** such as *is, are, was, were,* or *will be.*

> The star was *Glenna*. The star was *she*.

Object Pronouns: *me, us, you, him, her, it, them*

Use an **object pronoun** to take the place of a noun that is used as the **object of a verb** or the **object of a preposition** such as *above, after, around, at, before, behind, for, from, near, over, to, toward,* or *with.*

Direct Object: Liv ate the *cake*. Ian ate *it* too.

Indirect Object: Give *Erik* some popcorn. Give *him* some juice too.

Object of Preposition: The director pointed to *Carlo and Sandy*. The director pointed to *them*.

When an object pronoun is part of a **compound object**, make sure the pronoun is in the correct **form** and in the correct **order**.

> Miss Edelman gave *her* a raise.
> Miss Edelman gave *me* a raise.
> Miss Edelman gave *her and me* a raise.
> (not *she and I* or *me and her* or *her and I*)

Remember that a pronoun and its antecedent can be in different sentences.

> Let *Cassie* and *Hugh* leave early. Give *them* a pass.
> Hand the map to *Juan* and *Carly*. Then give *them* clear directions.

STUDY A MODEL

Bianca interviewed Anna for a column in the student paper. Read the interview.

Bianca: What happened at the chorus audition, and what's next?

Anna: Well, Fiona, Mark, and I auditioned. First, the conductor asked me to come to the stage. I felt faint. Mark admitted to us that the same thing had happened to him. During Fiona's audition, she looked relaxed and confident. Neither Mark nor I was surprised when the spot went to her. Without a doubt, the best singer is she. What's next? The next audition, I think.

Subject pronouns are red, and object pronouns are blue.

- The pronoun *I* is used as a subject, while the pronoun *me* is used as a direct object.

- The pronouns *us* and *him* are objects of prepositions.

- The pronoun *I* is part of the compound subject *Neither Mark nor I.*

- The pronoun *she* follows the linking verb *is.*

PRACTICE

A *Read the sentences. Label the underlined pronouns S for subject pronoun or O for object pronoun.*

1. <u>They</u> handed <u>her</u> a sheet of music.
2. She waved at <u>them</u>, and <u>they</u> waved back.
3. Recitals always make <u>me</u> nervous.
4. No problem is too difficult for <u>us</u>.
5. Would <u>you</u> please run an errand for <u>me</u>?
6. <u>He</u> applied glue, and <u>it</u> fixed the burst pipe.
7. Give the banner to <u>him</u> and <u>me</u>.
8. Of all the runners, the fastest are Jake and <u>I</u>.

B *Read each sentence. Rewrite the sentence, using the correct pronoun(s) to complete it.*

1. Pilar and Ted told (we, us) everything.
2. (She, Her) and (he, him) have won countless trophies.
3. The editors of the paper will be (he, him) and (I, me).
4. How should (we, us) deal with someone like (he, him)?
5. Will Ethan wait for you and (I, me)?
6. Did (he, him) ever call (she, her)?
7. Usually (we, us) get along with (they, them).
8. Some demonstrators passed (I, me) to walk behind (they, them).

C *Read the paragraph. Rewrite it, correcting the 8 pronouns that are used incorrectly.*

Inventors have designed scores of ingenious devices for we. Inventors are dreamers, but often them are admired. However, many other artists (and that includes I) are also dreamers, but we are not always admired. We are even considered lazy by some. They should understand that dreams are inventions, created by artists like we. Them on the street, him and her in the café, you and me passing by, are all dreamers and inventors.

Use a **subject pronoun** as a subject in a sentence or after a linking verb.
Use an **object pronoun** as a direct or indirect object or as the object of a preposition.

WRITE

Write an imaginary interview with a celebrity athlete or entertainer. Be sure to use correct pronouns.

Writing Tip
Never use the word *them* as an adjective.
Incorrect:
Please hand me *them* papers.
Correct:
Please hand me *those* papers.
Please hand *them* to me.

INTERROGATIVE AND RELATIVE PRONOUNS

THINK ABOUT

Use an **interrogative pronoun** *(who, whom, whose, which, what)* to ask a question.

who   *Who* wrote this science-fiction story?

whom   *Whom* did the detectives accuse of the crime?

whose   This territory is *whose*?

which   *Which* is the best solution?

what   *What* did the reviewer say about this story?

Use a **relative pronoun** *(who, whom, whose, which, that)* to introduce a group of words that has a subject and a verb and that describes a noun or pronoun in the sentence.

who   The people ***who*** *live here* are our friends.

whom   The jockey was someone ***whom*** *we knew.*

whose   This is the boy ***whose*** *glasses broke.*

which   The rain, ***which*** *we need,* delayed the game.

that   The cap ***that*** *I purchased* has earflaps.

- Remember to use **who** and **whom** correctly. Use **who** as a subject, and use **whom** as an object.

    Who is that terrifying character?
    Who has read the book by Dickens?
    Who said that?
    The actor *who* played that part has retired.
    About *whom* are you speaking?
    To *whom* did you give the book?
    After *whom* will you perform?
    I've heard from everyone *whom* I invited.

- Use **commas** to set off a group of words that is **not essential** to the meaning of the sentence.

    My friend, ***who*** *lives next door,* plays baseball.
    My promise, ***which*** *I now regret,* still holds.

    (The words in italics are not essential to the meaning of the sentences.)

- Do not **use commas** to set off a group of words that is **essential** to the meaning of the sentence.

    The girl ***who*** *lives next door* is my friend.
    The promise ***that*** *I made* still holds.

    (The words in italics are essential to the meaning of the sentences.)

STUDY A MODEL

Read the question-and-answer passage telling about the dictionary game.

What are the rules of this dictionary game? A lead player selects a challenging word from the dictionary, spells the word, and writes down its actual definition. The other players write down definitions that they make up. The leader reads a sentence that contains the word and then reads each of the definitions, which have been mixed together. The players vote for the definition that they think is the true one. Who wins points? Players whose definitions are chosen get one point per vote. The player who first guesses the actual definition gets three points.

Interrogative pronouns are red, and relative pronouns are blue.

The interrogative pronoun *What* introduces a question.

The relative pronoun *that* introduces a group of words that is essential to the meaning of the sentence. No commas are used around the group of words.

Notice that a comma is used before the group of words *which have been mixed together.* This group of words gives more information about the definitions, but it isn't essential to the basic meaning of the sentence.

The relative pronoun *whose* introduces a group of words that describes *Players.* Within the group of words, *whose* describes *definitions.*

12

PRACTICE

A *Read each sentence. Write the interrogative pronoun and label it* **I**, *or write the relative pronoun and label it* **R**.

1. What is the symbol of the Lionel Cab Company?
2. Is he the man who invented the lion's head trademark?
3. Which is the largest fleet of cabs in the city?
4. Whom did the customers vote the most courteous driver?
5. Use this signal, which is used for hailing cabs.
6. Whose is considered the best-maintained vehicle?
7. Do you know the percentage that is standard for calculating a tip?

B *Write a relative pronoun to complete each sentence.*

1. Cricket, _____ is an English sport, is a mystery to me.
2. The fact _____ it resembles baseball is confusing.
3. The person _____ throws the ball is known as the bowler.
4. The person _____ job it is to hit the ball is the batsman.
5. The person _____ stands behind the wicket is the wicketkeeper.
6. The team _____ has the highest score wins.
7. To _____ shall I turn for more information?

C *Read the paragraph. Label each of the 10 underlined pronouns* **I** *for interrogative or* **R** *for relative.*

<u>Who</u> wrote *David Copperfield*? Charles Dickens wrote the novel in 1850. The plot, <u>which</u> reflects Dickens's own life, is about people <u>who</u> faced great difficulties. <u>What</u> happened in Dickens's early life? His father was kind, but he was a man <u>who</u> could not support his family. Dickens's mother made the young boy work in a factory <u>that</u> was infested with rats. The working conditions, <u>which</u> were dreadful, shocked him. Later Dickens wrote about conditions <u>that</u> caused human misery. <u>Which</u> of Dickens's several novels is the greatest? Every reader <u>whom</u> you ask will have a different answer.

An **interrogative pronoun** introduces a question. A **relative pronoun** introduces a group of words that describe.

WRITE

Write a question-and-answer passage that gives instructions for doing something. Use interrogative and relative pronouns correctly.

Writing Tip

In your writing, use the relative pronoun *which* to introduce a group of words that is not essential to the meaning of the sentence.

- The final clue, **which** was very subtle, cracked the case.

Use the relative pronoun *that* to introduce a group of works that is essential to the meaning of the sentence.

- The team **that** cracked the case celebrated the victory.

THINK ABOUT

The word *reflexive* means "bending back." A **reflexive pronoun** reflects the action of the verb back to the subject.

They bought *themselves* lunch.

They and *themselves* are both involved in the action of the verb *bought*.

A reflexive pronoun ends in *-self* or *-selves*.

Singular	**Plural**
myself	ourselves
yourself	yourselves
himself, herself, itself	themselves

- A reflexive pronoun can be used as a **direct object, indirect object,** or **object of a preposition**.

Direct Object: I nominated *myself* for office.
Indirect Object: Jan bought *himself* a present.
Object of Preposition: We count on *ourselves*.

- Do not use a reflexive pronoun where a subject pronoun belongs.

  Incorrect: My friends and *myself* sing.
  Correct: My friends and *I* sing.

- Do not use a reflexive pronoun where an object pronoun belongs.

  Incorrect: Choose my brother and *myself*.
  Correct: Choose my brother and *me*.

- Do not use *hisself, themself, theirself, theirselves,* or *ourself*. These are not words.

An **intensive pronoun** is a reflexive pronoun that emphasizes or intensifies a **subject**. An intensive pronoun usually directly follows the subject. Because an intensive pronoun does not change the meaning of the sentence, it could be removed.

Nikki herself made the bookshelf.
The *paragraph itself* is not well written.
Did *Dwayne* write the script *himself*?

STUDY A MODEL

Read this conversational passage from a do-it-yourself home improvement handbook.

If you convince **yourself** to take on a home-improvement project, first devise a simple plan. Many times I **myself** have had to figure out the best way to get a job done. Trial and error have taught me that it's all in the planning. The work **itself** is usually not very difficult. Yet, many people convince **themselves** that they aren't handy. You should tell **yourself** what my cousin tells **himself**, "I AM handy." Then let **yourself** go!

> *Reflexive pronouns are blue, and intensive pronouns are red.*

◄ The reflexive pronoun *yourself* is a direct object and reflects the action of the verb *convince* back to the subject *you*. The words *you* and *yourself* refer to the same person.

◄ The intensive pronoun *itself* gives emphasis to the subject *work*, but *itself* could be removed from the sentence without changing the meaning.

◄ The reflexive pronoun *yourself* reflects action back to the subject *you*.

PRACTICE

A *Read each sentence. Write the reflexive pronoun that refers back to the underlined subject.*

1. The <u>motorist</u> found herself on an unfamiliar road.
2. Did <u>you</u> burn yourself on the charcoal grill?
3. <u>Alec</u> deceived himself about the quality of the used car.
4. <u>We</u> settled ourselves comfortably by the hotel pool.
5. <u>I</u> was proud of myself for memorizing the dialogue.
6. The <u>roses</u> twined themselves around the columns.
7. The <u>problem</u> did not lend itself to a simple solution.

B *Write a reflexive pronoun or an intensive pronoun to complete each sentence.*

1. Chen ___(intensive)___ programmed the video cassette recorder.
2. Have you ever programmed a VCR by ___(reflexive)___ ?
3. Some people tape favorite television programs for ___(reflexive)___ .
4. Chen played vacation and graduation videos that he made by ___(reflexive)___ .
5. Chen's sister ___(intensive)___ prefers to watch horror videos.
6. The VCR clock ___(intensive)___ is still a mystery to Chen.

C *Read the paragraph. Write the 9 pronouns that correctly complete the paragraph.*

Nick and (I, myself) put together the model speedboat (ourself, ourselves). Nick (hisself, himself) is an excellent model-builder. He explained each step as he demonstrated it to (myself, me). I was proud to assist Nick, (himself, myself). The finished model was beautifully assembled, and Nick and I were very proud of (ourself, ourselves). Later my sisters wanted us to help (themselves, them) build one. Eventually, they built one (themselves, theirselves). In the end, they thanked (us, ourselves) for the inspiration.

A **reflexive pronoun** reflects the action of the verb back to the subject.
An **intensive pronoun** is a reflexive pronoun that emphasizes or intensifies a subject.

WRITE

Write a conversational passage describing a job you think you'd like to have. Be sure to use reflexive and intensive pronouns correctly.

Writing Tip

In your writing, you also can use **demonstrative pronouns**, which replace nouns and point out someone or something specific. The demonstrative pronouns are *this, that, these,* and *those.*

- *This is the best bike in the shop.*
- *Is that the book you read?*
- *These are Silvio's favorite plants.*
- *Did you make those for the party?*

VERB TENSES

THINK ABOUT

It is important to use correct **verb tenses**, as well as exact verbs, in your writing. Verbs express action or tell something about a subject. Verb tenses express **time**.

You often use *present, past, or future tenses*. Sometimes you need to use **present, past,** or **future perfect tenses** to tell when something happened. These perfect tenses are formed by combining an auxiliary, or helping, verb with a past participle.

The **present perfect tense** refers to something that occurred at some indefinite time in the past or that began sometime in the past and continues in the present. To form the present perfect, combine the auxiliary verb *has* or *have* with the *past participle*.

Present	Past	Past Participle
bring	brought	brought
do	did	done
fly	flew	flown
go	went	gone
grow	grew	grown
hear	heard	heard
see	saw	seen
wake	woke	woken

Present Perfect Verbs in Sentences:
Ari *has been* a doctor for years.
We *have seen* that movie.
Have you *heard* this song before?

The **past perfect tense** refers to something that happened in the past before a specific time or event in the past. To form the past perfect, combine the auxiliary verb *had* with the *past participle*.

Past Participles: ripened; grown
Past Perfect Verbs in Sentences:
The tomato *had ripened* before I picked it.
Riva *had grown* an inch before school started.

The **future perfect tense** refers to something that will be completed by a specific time or event in the future. To form the future perfect, combine the auxiliary verb *will have* with the *past participle*.

Past Participles: solved; finished
Future Perfect Verbs in Sentences:
By tomorrow we *will have solved* the case.
Will you *have finished* the sets by show time?

STUDY A MODEL

Read this press release about a creative team.

> For decades, the world has admired the author/illustrator team of Joe and Ilse. For some time, people have speculated that the two might never collaborate again. Then word trickled out that just before leaving on her summer vacation, Ilse had agreed to illustrate Joe's next book. The pair had thought they would begin work this week. Then by next June, editors will have reviewed the text. Finally, by July, the publisher will have approved the design. Then everyone will know that Joe and Ilse are back!

Present perfect verbs are red, past perfect verbs are blue, and future perfect verbs are green.

 In the first sentence, *has admired* is in the present perfect tense, referring to something that began in the past and continues in the present (admiring).

 Had agreed is in the past perfect, referring to something that happened (agreeing) in the past before something else happened in the past (Ilse's going on vacation).

 Will have reviewed is in the future perfect, referring to something (reviewing) that will be completed by a certain time in the future (next June).

PRACTICE

A *Read each sentence. Label the underlined verb Present Perfect, Past Perfect, or Future Perfect.*

1. The yoga instructor <u>has stressed</u> the importance of concentration.
2. Raúl <u>had bought</u> the shirt before the sale was announced.
3. The birds <u>will have finished</u> the food by tomorrow morning.
4. Grandmother <u>has exercised</u> daily for fifty years.
5. <u>Will</u> Kit <u>have received</u> the report by next week's meeting?
6. Kylie mentioned that Erik <u>had heard</u> dozens of CDs.

B *In each sentence, write the verb in the tense indicated.*

1. By next month, they (determine, *future perfect*) the book's design.
2. They (consider, *present perfect*) our readers' interests for years.
3. By next fall, Helen (complete, *future perfect*) the text?
4. He (select, *past perfect*) the sites before the photo shoot.
5. You and other photographers (travel, *present perfect*) to distant places.
6. They (see, *past perfect*) our work before yesterday's show.

C *Read the paragraph. Change each of the 5 underlined verbs to the present perfect, past perfect, or future perfect tense. Use the tense that makes the most sense in the context.*

You know that action photographers <u>develop</u> quick reflexes when they capture special moments on film. Timing always is a major technical challenge in this art form. In the past, wildlife photographers <u>track</u> their subjects first. Only after they <u>calculated</u> the animal's rate of movement could the picture be taken. If the animal was dangerous or fast, they traveled alongside in moving vehicles while taking pictures. More recently, video cameras <u>made</u> it easier for amateur action photographers to achieve impressive results. By the time I'm 25, I hope I <u>produce</u> a successful nature film.

The **present perfect tense**, **past perfect**, and **future perfect tenses** of verbs are formed by combining an auxiliary verb with a past participle.

WRITE

Write a press release about a real or imaginary event. Use verb tenses correctly.

Writing Tip
Whenever possible, use exact verbs instead of vague, general verbs.

General	Exact
run:	dart, dash, gallop, race, sprint
talk:	babble, chatter, drone, jabber, rap, utter
think:	consider, contemplate, deliberate, ponder, reflect

SUBJECT-VERB AGREEMENT

THINK ABOUT

A **verb** must agree with its **subject** in **number**.

Use a **singular verb** with a singular subject.
> The *student* **takes** notes.
> *He* **writes** novels.

Use a **plural verb** with a plural subject.
> *Donors* **give** money.
> *We* **give** our time.

Use a **plural verb** with a **compound subject** joined by *and* or by *both . . . and*.
> *Jon and Ray* **are** cousins. *Both she and I* **race**.

Use a **singular verb** with a **compound subject** modified by *each* or *every* or with a compound subject that is singular in meaning.
> *Each* cat and dog **is** healthy.
> *Fish and chips* always **makes** a good meal.

If a **compound subject** is joined by *or*, *neither . . . nor*, or *either . . . or*, the verb agrees with the **closer subject**.
> *Pam's irises or her geranium* **wins**.
> *Either Marie or her brothers* **bake** on Fridays.

Make sure the subject and the verb agree when the **verb comes before the subject** in the sentence.
> Where **is** *Deena*?
> In the hall **sits** the *umbrella*.

Use a **singular verb** with most plural-form subjects that are singular in meaning.
> *Social studies* **lasts** an hour. *Two dollars* **is** the price.

Use a **plural verb** with subjects such as *glasses, pants, scissors,* or *binoculars*.
> *Glasses* **help** my eyes. The *binoculars* **are** strong.

Collective nouns such as *crowd, jury, public,* and *team* can be either singular or plural. Use a **singular verb** when the collective noun refers to the group as a whole.
> Our *band* **performs** at every game.

Use a **plural verb** when the collective noun refers to the individual members of the group.
> The *children* **exit** one at a time.

Make sure a **verb** agrees with the **subject of the sentence**, *not* with a noun or a pronoun in a *separating phrase or clause*.
> The *players* on our team **strive** for excellence.
> *Lisa*, as well as her sisters, **plays** softball.

STUDY A MODEL

Read this paragraph from an article in an environmental magazine.

> The redwood trees of California are the tallest living things in the world. The largest tree reaches 364 feet! Redwood trees are invulnerable to insects and rot. Because of this, redwood lumber is highly valued. The public, however, demands sensible harvesting, and the logging industry follows specific guidelines. Each harvest of the trees requires careful planning. At the same time, both scientists and environmentalists explore better methods of growing redwoods. Are redwoods worth protecting? Yes, they are.

Singular subjects and verbs are red. Plural subjects and verbs are blue.

Notice in the first sentence that redwood *trees* is a plural subject with the plural verb *are*, even though the singular word *California* is closer to the verb.

Redwood lumber is a singular subject with the singular verb *is*.

Public and *harvest* are both singular subjects with singular verbs.

Both scientists and environmentalists is a compound subject joined by *both . . . and*.

Here the verb *Are* comes before the subject *redwoods*. Both are plural.

PRACTICE

A *Read each sentence. Write the verb that agrees with the underlined subject.*

1. Our <u>group</u> (wants, want) equal time.
2. <u>Both James and she</u> (campaigns, campaign) for me.
3. This <u>team</u> of athletes (gets, get) a trophy at the end of the season.
4. The <u>members</u> of that family (is, are) close.
5. Neither <u>my dad nor my brothers</u> (enjoys, enjoy) baseball.
6. Those <u>trousers</u> (looks, look) sloppy on me.
7. In the forest (is, are) several <u>footpaths</u>.

B *Read each sentence. Write the subject and the verb with which it agrees. Include each or both . . . and in subjects as needed. Write S if the subject and verb are singular. Write P if they are plural.*

1. Gymnastics is my favorite sport.
2. Gymnasts wear special clothes.
3. Most practical are stretchy clothes.
4. Each player on my team wears the same color.
5. Team uniforms are expensive.
6. Each gymnast and coach needs a leotard.
7. This pair of shorts fits a slender person.
8. Both Kate and Dustin compete.

C *Read the paragraph. Rewrite it, correcting the 8 errors in subject–verb agreement.*

Both Horst and his sister Addie looks forward to their canoe trip to the lighthouse. This canoe trip, unlike others, are an annual event. Neither their dad nor their grandparents are expecting anyone to be at the lighthouse. Relatively unknown is the joys of this island. Twelve hours seem like a long time to be alone on the island, but it is never enough. The hours of the day passes quickly. Each adult and child explore the island. At six o'clock, the group pack up and paddle reluctantly home.

A **verb** must agree with its **subject** in **number**.

WRITE

Write a paragraph about an environmental topic. Write in the present tense, and make sure all subjects and verbs agree.

Writing Tip
Sometimes a subject of a sentence is a **verb form** that is being **used as a noun**. These subjects are singular and take a singular verb.

*Sleeping **is** my new hobby.*
*Is **copying** allowed?*
*To win **was** their goal.*
*To complain **is** useless.*

MORE SUBJECT-VERB AGREEMENT

THINK ABOUT

Subjects and verbs must agree in number. Sometimes a subject is an indefinite pronoun. An **indefinite pronoun** refers to a *person, place, or thing that is not specific.*

- When a **singular indefinite pronoun** is the **subject** of a sentence, use a **singular verb**.

  Singular indefinite pronouns include *another, anybody, anyone, anything, each, either, everybody, everyone, everything, much, neither, nobody, no one, other, nothing, one, somebody, someone,* and *something.*

  *Someone **has** that website address.*

  *No one in my class **knows** the time.*

  *Nothing that we do **stops** that player!*

  ***Is** something wrong with your voice?*

- When a **plural indefinite pronoun** is the **subject** of a sentence, use a **plural verb**.

  Plural indefinite pronouns include *both, few, many, ones, others,* and *several.*

  *Both **are** on vacation.*
  *Few **respond** to our ads.*
  *Many **eat** breakfast here.*
  *Several **meet** outside school.*

- The indefinite pronouns *all, any, more, most, none,* and *some* used as a subject take **either a singular or a plural verb**, depending on the object of the preposition that follows the subject.

  *All of the **paint** is white.*

  *Most of the **food** is gone.*

  *All of the **walls** are white.*

  *Most of the **homes** are empty.*

STUDY A MODEL

Read this passage about the benefits of therapy animals.

Therapy animals are like friends to their owners, and usually both benefit from the relationship. Many of these animals, usually dogs or cats, need little training. They are chosen because they are friendly and calm, and they love being around people. Something about therapy with animals makes others feel better.

Doctors sometimes see therapy animals at work. Most of these professionals observe that patients feel better after the visit. Some think the animals actually heal the sick. Each doctor feels that therapy animals are special.

Singular indefinite pronoun subjects and singular verbs are red. Plural indefinite pronoun subjects and plural verbs are blue.

Notice that the indefinite pronoun *Many* refers to the plural noun *animals* and agrees with the plural verb *need.*

In this sentence, *Something* is singular and agrees with the singular verb *makes* even though the plural word *animals* comes directly before the verb. *Animals* is the object of a separating phrase.

Notice that *Most* and *Some* are plural, but *Each* is singular.

PRACTICE

A *Read each sentence. Write the verb that agrees with the underlined subject.*

1. Everyone (agrees, agree) that his script is a success.
2. (Is, Are) all of the students late for class?
3. Nobody (chooses, choose) to react hastily.
4. Several of her designs (is, are) very popular.
5. Neither (has, have) a new uniform.
6. Many (knows, know) the secret of the ancient tomb.
7. Much (is, are) still unknown about the strangers.

B *Read each sentence. Write the subject and then write the verb in parentheses that agrees with the subject.*

1. Many of the players (arrives, arrive) early for games.
2. (Is, Are) each of the reporters present?
3. None of the band members (likes, like) practice in the rain.
4. Many of our classes (is, are) already full.
5. Few (doubt, doubts) the supervisor's decision.
6. (Is, Are) all of the pies gone?
7. Both (pose, poses) a challenge.

C *Read the paragraph. Rewrite it, correcting the 7 errors in subject–verb agreement.*

At noon, many factory employees takes one hour for lunch and relaxation. Most of the noisy machines shuts down at that time. Most of the workers leave, but some lingers on the grounds or beside the mill pond. Others prefers a stroll around the pond. One of my lunchtime pleasures are to sketch the people nearby. None of my pastimes gives me more satisfaction than this. After all these years, most of my co-workers is used to my creative pursuits. Fortunately, none seem to mind!

> An **indefinite pronoun** subject must agree with its verb in number.

WRITE

Write a passage about the benefits of something you believe in. Use the present tense and make sure any indefinite pronouns and their verbs agree.

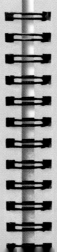

Writing Tip

Avoid **double negatives** in your writing. Double negatives usually don't say what you intend to say.

- **Double Negative:** Nobody knows nothing.
- **Intended Meaning:** Nobody knows anything.
- **Actual Meaning:** Everybody knows something.

ADJECTIVES

THINK ABOUT

Adjectives can make your writing more specific, informative, and interesting. An **adjective** is a word that modifies, or describes, a noun or a pronoun by telling *what kind, how many,* or *which one.*

What Kind: Sam does *neat* work. Use the *fresh* eggs.
How Many: I have *several* hats. I lost *one* sock.
Which One(s): *That* sprinter won. *Those* shoes fit.
Enter the *first* door.

- Adjectives can come *before* or *after* the noun or pronoun they modify.

  Who ate *four* sandwiches?
  Amy, *young* and *energetic,* ran home.

- Most adjectives have **three degrees of comparison**. The **positive degree** makes no comparison. The **comparative degree** compares two nouns or pronouns. Form it by adding *er* to most short adjectives or the word *more* or *less* to longer ones. The **superlative degree** compares three or more nouns or pronouns. Form it by adding *est* to most short adjectives or the word *most* or *least* to longer ones.

Positive Degree	Comparative Degree	Superlative Degree
clear	clearer	clearest
confident	more confident	most confident
miserable	less miserable	least miserable

- *Bad, good,* and *many* have special forms for the comparative and superlative degrees.

Positive	Comparative	Superlative
bad	worse	worst
good	better	best
many	more	most

- Adjectives such as *circular* and *unique* do not have a comparative or superlative degree. For example, a shape cannot be *more* circular or *most* circular.

- Avoid *double comparisons*. Never use *more* or *less* with adjectives that end in *er*. Never use *most* or *least* with adjectives that end in *est*.

Incorrect: *more faster*   **Correct:** *faster*
Incorrect: *most funniest*   **Correct:** *funniest*

STUDY A MODEL

Read the following description from maritime history.

In 1628, a crowd, noisy and eager, gathered in Stockholm, Sweden. The Wasa was leaving on her maiden voyage. Those people had never seen a more impressive spectacle. Soon, however, a powerful gust of wind struck the ship. Despite the most frantic efforts of the crew, the vessel sank. For years, many people tried to recover valuable items from the wreck. In 1663, a special chamber enabled divers to recover fifty-three cannons. In 1956, television viewers looked on as the ship was lifted from the sea. Was this sight less awesome than the launch? Many said no.

Adjectives are red.

- In the first sentence, the adjectives *noisy* and *eager* both describe *crowd,* telling *what kind* of crowd.

- *Those* modifies *people,* telling *which ones.*

- *More impressive* is comparative, while *most frantic* is superlative.

- *Many* tells *how many* people.

- The adjective *fifty-three* tells how many cannons. *Television* tells *what kind* of viewers.

- *Less awesome* is comparative.

PRACTICE

A *Read each sentence. Write the noun that is modified by the underlined adjective. Then write the adjective and label it* **What Kind, How Many,** *or* **Which One**(s).

1. Rena plunged into the <u>turbulent</u> water.
2. Only the <u>most passionate</u> love of swimming could explain her zeal.
3. Sun dappled the water as she swam the <u>nine</u> laps.
4. That day the water was unusually <u>calm</u>.
5. Rena struggled to maintain her <u>strenuous</u> pace!
6. Were <u>those</u> limbs going to last?
7. Amazingly, Rena swam for <u>thirty</u> minutes.
8. Rena slowed during the <u>last</u> lap, but she finished!

B *Read each sentence. Write the adjective or adjectives that modify the underlined noun. Do not include articles (a, an, the).*

1. The sun blazed in a clear, blue <u>sky</u>.
2. The many <u>spectators</u> crowded the beach.
3. These <u>divers</u> are very strong.
4. A sincere <u>instructor</u> repeated the rules.
5. All <u>divers</u> listened attentively.
6. The cool, calm <u>water</u> soothed the divers.
7. They felt that this was the most peaceful <u>place</u> of all.

C *Read the paragraph. Rewrite it, correcting the 8 errors in comparison.*

Of the four groups of reptiles alive today, alligators and crocodiles are the closer relatives to dinosaurs. Both reptiles live in the most warmest tropical climates. Alligators have more broader, shortest snouts than crocodiles do. Crocodiles are small and thin than alligators. When it is captured, the crocodile is fiercest than the alligator is. Which do you think is the most boldest?

An **adjective** modifies, or describes, a noun or a pronoun by telling *what kind, how many,* or *which one.*

WRITE

Write a description of a favorite place. It may be an exotic travel destination or a place you visit every day. Use adjectives to make the place come alive for readers.

Writing Tip
Keep in mind that a word can be **more than one part of speech,** depending on how you use it in a sentence.

- Where's the *cat?* (noun)
- Let's buy a *cat* toy. (adjective)
- I like your new *plants.* (noun)
- You should *plant* corn here. (verb)
- My mom wants a *plant* stand. (adjective)

ADVERBS

THINK ABOUT

Adverbs can make your writing more precise, informative, and descriptive. An **adverb** modifies a *verb* by telling *how, when,* or *where.* An **adverb** modifies an *adjective* or another *adverb* by telling *how much* or *to what extent.* An adverb often, but not always, ends in *ly.*

How: The puppy *ate* **quickly**.
When: We *will meet* **someday**.
Where: The evening bus *stops* **here**.
How Much: We were **extremely** *lucky*.
To What Extent: I *ran* **somewhat** *faster*.

- An adverb can come either *before* or *after* a verb that it modifies.

  They *left* **quietly**. They **quietly** *left*.

- An adverb can come at the *beginning* or at the *end* of a sentence.

  Sometimes I *work* at home.
  I *work* at home **sometimes**.

  Use a comma after an introductory adverb if you want readers to pause.

  Fortunately, I was at home.

- An adverb can come between the main verb and the auxiliary, or helping, verb in a verb phrase.

  Chloe *could* **almost** *see* the island.

- Like adjectives, most adverbs have three degrees of comparison: **positive, comparative,** and **superlative**.

  To form the **comparative** degree, add *er* or the word *more* or *less.* To form the **superlative** degree, add *est* or the word *most* or *least.*

Positive	Comparative	Superlative
early	earlier	earliest
rapidly	more rapidly	most rapidly
courageously	less courageously	least courageously

  Well and *badly* have special forms for the comparative and superlative degrees.

Positive	Comparative	Superlative
well	better	best
badly	worse	worst

- Avoid double comparisons. Do not use *more* or *most* with adverbs that end in *er* or *est.*

  Incorrect: He ran *more slower*.
  Correct: He ran *slower*.

STUDY A MODEL

Read this entry from Nellie's diary.

> The school concert is soon, and I am very nervous. Quite foolishly, I let the fear of performing get to me. Then I remind myself of several things. First, my teacher has often praised my progress. Second, my family and friends wholeheartedly celebrate my music. Third, I am a very good player. This year I have certainly practiced more diligently than last year. If I remember these things and don't let fear lead me astray, I might play better than I have ever played. I might actually enjoy the concert.

Adverbs are red.

Notice that the adverb *very* modifies the adjective *nervous*, and the adverb *Quite* modifies another adverb, *foolishly*.

The adverb *often* modifies the verb *has praised*, telling *when*. Also notice that *often* comes between the helping verb *has* and the main verb *praised*.

More diligently is in the comparative degree.

Better is also in the comparative degree.

24

PRACTICE

A *Read the 9 sentences and write the adverbs.*

1. Gerardo bakes pumpernickel bread daily.
2. Scientists now determine the ages of meteorites.
3. Sometimes we allow ourselves to daydream.
4. Heat can be more rapidly lost through the head than through the feet.
5. News of the sale spread faster than we had expected.
6. The second wave rose higher than the first.
7. The author was truly loved by her readers.
8. The butler glowered very coldly at the dog's dirty feet.
9. Of all the swimmers, Kristen swam the fastest.

B *Read each sentence. Write the word or words modified by the underlined adverb.*

1. The command module <u>continuously</u> orbited the moon.
2. <u>Suddenly</u> the astronauts paused.
3. The testing of the equipment had been <u>very</u> thorough.
4. The astronauts were <u>extremely</u> careful with the equipment.
5. The lunar module landed <u>perfectly</u>.
6. On the moon the astronauts performed <u>better</u> than ever before.
7. The media has <u>highly</u> praised the astronauts for their work.

C *Read the paragraph. Write the 10 adverbs and the word or words that each modifies.*

Alexander Pope has long been considered one of the greatest English poets of his time. He is often remembered for his satire. By the age of twenty-three, Pope was already quite famous. His fame had spread very rapidly. His *An Essay on Criticism* had solidly placed him in literary circles. Some of Pope's contemporaries intensely disliked him because he often attacked them in his poetry, but Pope's popularity survived, as it survives today.

An **adverb** is a word that modifies, or describes, a *verb*, an *adjective*, or another *adverb*.

WRITE

Write a diary entry describing a meaningful event. Use adverbs to bring the event to life.

Writing Tip
- Avoid using illogical or incomplete **comparisons**.
  Incorrect:
  My computer is faster than Vanessa.
  Correct:
  My computer is faster than **Vanessa's**.
- Some words can be **adverbs** or **prepositions**.
  The men went **below** (adv).
  The sun went **below** the horizon (prep).

ADJECTIVES AND ADVERBS

THINK ABOUT

Adjectives and adverbs are both modifiers.

- **Adjectives** modify, or describe, *nouns* or *pronouns*.

  Have you ever seen such a ***spectacular*** *cactus*?
  The box was filled with ***old*** *newspapers*.

  When we appeared, *he* was ***speechless***.

- **Adverbs** modify *verbs, adjectives,* or other *adverbs*.

  The dog *raced* ***downstairs***.

  "He is ***absolutely*** *wrong*," said Jacob.

  The stars shone ***quite*** *brightly*.

- Adjectives and adverbs are sometimes confused when they follow verbs.

  Adjectives often follow **linking verbs** such as *is, are, was, become, seem, appear, look, sound, smell, taste,* or *feel*.
     Gus *is* ***happy***. Tia *seems* ***responsible***.

  Adverbs often follow **action verbs**.
     Gus *smiles* ***happily***. Tia *behaves* ***responsibly***.

- The words *bad, good, real,* and *sure* are **adjectives**.
     Ten ribs have ***bad*** *fractures*.
     The hikers had a ***good*** *day*.
     Is that a ***real*** *diamond*?
     Are *you* ***sure***?

- The words *badly, really,* and *surely* are **adverbs**.
     Two ribs are ***badly*** *bruised*.
     The newcomers are ***really*** *frightened*.
     We ***surely*** *plan* to win.

- The word *well* is usually an **adverb**, except when it describes a state of health. Then it works as an **adjective**.

     This machine *works* ***well*** in the fields.

     Henry *swam* ***well*** in practice.

     Shawna still doesn't *feel* ***well***.

     I *feel* ***well*** now.

STUDY A MODEL

Read this paragraph about hot-air balloons.

> Before it rises skyward, a hot-air balloon must be filled with helium. The odorless gas is quite light. During inflation, the brilliantly colorful balloon fills with gas. It expands almost imperceptibly, until it has become rotund. As the balloon inflates fully, it lifts easily off the ground. The pilot, who stands in a basket beneath the balloon, releases sand gradually. The balloon becomes lighter. Then the balloon really flies!

Words in red are adjectives.
Words in blue are adverbs.

In the first sentence, *skyward* is an adverb that modifies the verb *rises*.

Brilliantly is an adverb modifying the adjective *colorful*, which modifies the noun *balloon*.

Almost is an adverb modifying another adverb, *imperceptibly*.

Rotund is an adjective modifying the pronoun *it*.

Lighter is an adjective modifying *balloon*.

Really is an adverb modifying the verb *flies*.

PRACTICE

A *Read the sentences. Label each of the 14 underlined words* **Adjective** *or* **Adverb.**

1. They are <u>usually</u> <u>late</u> for meetings.
2. The tourists have <u>greatly</u> admired the <u>beautiful</u> gardens of Versailles.
3. "No place should feel <u>so</u> <u>cold</u>!"
4. The sunrise is <u>very</u> <u>lovely</u>, but the sunset is <u>lovelier</u>.
5. We waited <u>three</u> hours for a <u>really</u> <u>bad</u> dinner.
6. He followed the <u>installation</u> instructions <u>well</u>.

B *Read each sentence. Write the adjective or adverb that correctly completes it.*

1. Today's assembly (sure, surely) could win a booby prize.
2. (Sad, Sadly), this is the final meet of the year.
3. I ran (well, good) at first, but then my legs began to ache.
4. To float, a balloon needs to be (full, fully) inflated with helium.
5. Is your summer job a (sure, surely) thing?
6. The crowd appreciates players who skate (good, well).
7. They could have reacted (bad, badly), but they were good sports.
8. Brandon sat down because he didn't feel (good, well).

C *Read the paragraph. Write the 10 words that correctly complete the paragraph.*

The Underground Railroad wasn't a (real, really) railroad. It wasn't even underground. It was a complex series of (secret, secretly) routes and hiding places. Through this system, slaves made their way (safe, safely) to the North. For over two hundred years, the slaves had had no (actual, actually) freedom. Finally, in (large, largely) numbers, they were running away from (terrible, terribly) conditions in the South. They (true, truly) believed they would find freedom in the North. Through the Underground Railroad, many traveled (slow, slowly) toward their (true, truly) goal. Though the trip was (treacherous, treacherously), thousands made it!

Adjectives and **adverbs** are modifiers. Adjectives modify *nouns* or *pronouns*. Adverbs modify *verbs*, *adjectives*, or other *adverbs*.

WRITE

Write a paragraph about something you own and would like to sell. Use adjectives and adverbs to realistically describe the item.

Writing Tip

A **prepositional phrase** can act as an **adjective**.

I wore the sweater with the stripes.
(tells *which one*)

A **prepositional phrase** can act as an **adverb**.

The mouse ran across the floor.
(tells *where*)

HOMOPHONES

THINK ABOUT

Homophones are words that sound alike but have different meanings and spellings. They are sometimes confused in writing. The following are some common homophones.

allowed, aloud — You are *allowed* to read *aloud*.

council, counsel — The mayor offered her *counsel* to the town-planning *council*.

heard, herd — They *heard* the thundering buffalo *herd*.

hole, whole — My *whole* sandwich fell down that *hole*!

knot, not — That *knot* is *not* tied correctly.

know, no — I *know* there is *no* soup left.

principal, principle — The *principal* described the *principle* of fairness.

right, write — My friend begged me to *write* *right* back.

scene, seen — Have you *seen* the entire second *scene*?

stationary, stationery — Holding the flowers *stationary*, Li drew a picture of them for her *stationery*.

to, too, two — *Two* miles is not *too* far *to* swim, for a dolphin.

wait, weight — I can *wait* to check my *weight*.

way, weigh — This is no *way* to *weigh* a cat.

Some homophone pairs include a **contraction**.

it's, its — See that puppy? *It's* chasing *its* tail.

their, there, they're — *They're* lucky *their* cab stopped *there*.

you're, your — *You're* the leader of *your* team.

who's, whose — *Who's* going to say *whose* turn comes next?

STUDY A MODEL

Read this version of a note from one explorer to another.

My dear Livingstone,

You're an intrepid explorer, while I am more **stationary**. I admit that I envy your adventures. Now, on **stationery** I write that I, too, have **seen** a remarkable scene! My **principal** destination is **too** far **to** walk but less than **two** dozen miles from home. My spot is **not** a place that many **know**; **their** stomachs would **knot** down **there**. Can you guess? All **right**, on **principle** I shall reveal **its** locale. **It's** Hidden Cave, where I've been spelunking, or caving.

Your friend, Stanley

> **Homophones are red.**

◄ Notice that the homophone *You're* is the contraction of the pronoun *you* and the verb *are*, while *your* is a possessive pronoun.

◄ *Seen* is a verb, while *scene* is a noun.

◄ *Too* is an adverb, *to* is a part of a verb phrase, and *two* is an adjective.

◄ *Their* shows possession, while *there* functions as an adverb.

◄ *Its* shows possession, while *It's* is a contraction of *It is*.

PRACTICE

A *Read each sentence. Rewrite the sentence, using the correct word(s) to complete it.*

1. The (principal, principle) gave awards to the students.
2. That (stationary, stationery) front is affecting our weather.
3. The (hole, whole) message was confusing to Samantha.
4. (To, Too, Two) days from now, I hope (to, too, two) be finished (to, too, two).
5. Which (way, weigh) did Armando go?
6. I want to join the student (council, counsel).
7. (Its, It's) not (right, write) that (their, there, they're) winning.

B *Read each sentence. Write the incorrect homophone correctly. If there is no error, write* **Correct.**

1. The principle of the school wants to meet with all the teachers.
2. On monogrammed stationery, he issued his statement.
3. The city counsel eventually voted to renovate the buildings.
4. The judge will counsel the district attorney about the procedure.
5. As a matter of principal, the attorney offered no opinion.
6. It's uncertain who's coat and hat these are.
7. "Your not going to get away with this," she said.

C *Read the paragraph. Write the 12 words that correctly complete the paragraph.*

Roxanne had (to, too, two) options: to accept the appointment to the student (council, counsel) or to decline. Roxanne didn't (know, no) whether her busy schedule (aloud, allowed) another commitment. She asked her father (to, too, two) (council, counsel) her. Her father said, "Because (your, you're) grades are good, I advise you to accept. Still, (your, you're) the one (who's, whose) the best judge of how to use (your, you're) time." Roxanne sat down and wrote on some white (stationary, stationery), "(It's, Its) my honor to accept the appointment."

Homophones are words that sound alike but have different meanings and spellings.

WRITE

Write a note telling a friend a few things that you would like to do, or do better, in your life. Make sure you spell any homophones correctly.

Writing Tips

People often quickly say the verb **have,** and it sounds like **of.** Make sure you don't write the preposition *of* when you mean *have.*

Incorrect: We should of called.

Correct: We should *have* called.

Similarly, make sure you don't write *then* when you mean *than. Then* refers to time, and *than* is used in comparisons.

Incorrect: This car is newer *then* that one.

Correct: This car is newer *than* that one.

SIMPLE, COMPOUND, AND COMPLEX SENTENCES

THINK ABOUT

In your writing, use different kinds of sentences: **simple, compound,** and **complex.**

- A **simple sentence** contains one **independent clause.** A clause is a group of words that has both a subject and a predicate. An **independent clause** expresses a complete thought and can stand alone.

  I sing.   Harry sings well.

  A **simple sentence,** which is one **independent clause,** may have a *compound subject* or a *compound predicate* and may contain *phrases.*

Simple Sentences:
Kerri and Nan ate lunch *before noon.*
The teacher *stood and introduced* herself *to everyone.*

- A **compound sentence** contains two or more **independent clauses** that are joined by a **comma** and a **coordinating conjunction** such as *and, but,* or *or.* Related clauses may also be joined by a **semicolon.**

Compound Sentences:
My brother uses a boat, **or** he sits on the dock.
I like fish; my dad does too.

- A **complex sentence** contains one **independent clause** and one or more **dependent clauses.**

A **dependent clause** is a group of words that has a subject and a predicate but does not express a complete thought and does not make sense alone. It requires an **independent clause** to complete its meaning. A dependent clause begins with a **relative pronoun** *(who, whom, whose, which, that)* or with a **subordinating conjunction** such as *after, although, as, as if, because, before, if, even if, since, so that, unless, until, when, whenever, where, wherever,* or *while.*

Dependent Clauses:
after we left the stadium (doesn't tell what happened)
which I appreciate (doesn't tell what is appreciated)

Complex Sentences:
After we left the stadium, we rode home. (Use a comma after a dependent clause that begins a sentence.)
I'll wait here *until the rain stops.* (no comma)

A **dependent clause** sometimes comes between the subject and the predicate of an **independent clause.**
Your help, *which I appreciate,* got the job done.
The person *who finishes first* wins movie tickets.

STUDY A MODEL

Read this entry in a student's journal.

I need help with this writing assignment! My teacher gave the class this huge assignment that must be done on Friday. While I have an active mind, topics for papers don't come easily. Not a single idea has popped into my head. Jeremy and Antoine have already finished their papers, but I haven't even begun. Although I work best under pressure, this is ridiculous. The clock is ticking, the paper is staring at me, and my mind is blank. Unless I get a better idea, which is not likely, I'll write about indecision!

 The first sentence is **simple;** it is one independent clause.

The second sentence is **complex,** with one independent clause and one essential dependent clause *(that must be done on Friday).*

The fifth sentence is **compound,** with two independent clauses joined by a comma and the conjunction *but.*

 The sixth sentence is **complex,** with one independent clause and one dependent clause, which introduces the sentence.

The eighth sentence is **complex,** with two dependent clauses. The second clause is not essential and is set off by commas.

PRACTICE

A *Read each clause. Label it **D** for dependent or **I** for independent.*

1. who create collages
2. it lasted six hours
3. although it was tasty
4. no proof exists
5. before dinner began
6. as the president spoke
7. since you insist
8. while I remained
9. crops could die
10. time was not allocated
11. whose hair was red
12. she waited

B *Read the sentences. Write the 5 dependent clauses and the 8 independent clauses.*

1. A baby horse is a colt; a baby kangaroo is a joey.
2. Although there may be a Loch Ness monster, no real proof exists.
3. Mt. St. Helens erupted and totally transformed its appearance.
4. Although this fruit is nutritious, it is sour.
5. If monsoons don't bring enough rainfall, the crops will die.
6. Corkboard and fiberboard provide the insulation that this house needs.
7. When he removed the pie from the oven, it was perfectly golden.

C *Read the paragraph. Label each of the 9 sentences **Simple**, **Compound**, or **Complex**.*

   Who made the first loaf of bread? No one really knows, but bread has been around for thousands of years. Even people who lived in caves long ago gathered grain. They cracked the grain open and found the tasty inner core. Although it was a time-consuming process, the people crushed the grain between stones, mixed it with water, and heated it. Some prehistoric bread that was unearthed by archaeologists contains bits of bone. Human skulls were also found at the site. Some of the skulls have teeth that are worn down. This bread was hard to make; it was also hard to chew!

A **simple sentence** contains one independent clause. A **compound sentence** contains two or more independent clauses, joined by a comma and a conjunction or by a semicolon. A **complex sentence** contains one independent clause and one or more dependent clauses.

WRITE

Write a journal entry about a challenging situation. Use simple, compound, and complex sentences correctly.

Writing Tip

Don't confuse a **compound sentence** (with two independent clauses) with a **simple sentence** (one independent clause) that has a compound predicate.

Compound Sentence:

Stacy and her mother shopped, and they had lunch.

Simple Sentence:

Stacy and her mother shopped and had lunch.

PLACING MODIFIERS IN SENTENCES

THINK ABOUT

To avoid confusion, place words, phrases, and clauses that are used as **modifiers** as close as possible to the words that they describe.

Unclear: The scarecrow frightened the birds on the stake.

Clear: The scarecrow *on the stake* frightened the birds.

Unclear: Mr. Mason talks every morning to the janitor, my new history teacher.

Clear: Mr. Mason, *my new history teacher,* talks every morning to the janitor.

Unclear: The clown waved at my cousin with the red nose.

Clear: The clown *with the red nose* waved at my cousin.

Unclear: In 1964 my grandpa bought his first car from Mr. Dixon, a Chevy.

Clear: In 1964 my grandpa bought his first car, *a Chevy,* from Mr. Dixon.

Unclear: Sue waved to the crowd crossing the finish line.

Clear: *Crossing the finish line,* Sue waved to the crowd.

Unclear: Newly polished, Sahar peered into the mirror.

Clear: Sahar peered into the *newly polished* mirror.

Unclear: Parrots are favorites of pet owners with colorful feathers.

Clear: Parrots *with colorful feathers* are favorites of pet owners.

Unclear: The picnickers ate the apple pie with relish.

Clear: *With relish,* the picnickers ate the apple pie.

The meaning of a sentence can change depending on the **placement** of a modifier.

Pedro will eat asparagus *only* with butter.
Pedro will *only* eat asparagus with butter.
Only Pedro eats asparagus with butter.

STUDY A MODEL

Read this excerpt from a biography of Hans Christian Andersen.

Hans Christian Andersen's stories, with their wisdom and humor, are read by millions. His early works, most of which are plays, are not widely known. The fairy tales that Andersen wrote later brought him fame. In one fairy tale, he drew upon his childhood experiences. Andersen, who was born in Denmark, had a difficult childhood. As a teenager, Andersen left school and worked. Jonas Collin, a friend, helped Andersen go back to school, the right place for the creative youth.

Modifiers are red.

Notice that the phrase *with their wisdom and humor* is appropriately placed next to *stories,* which it modifies.

The clause *that Andersen wrote later* follows *fairy tales,* which it modifies.

The phrase *a friend* modifies *Jonas Collin,* defining him.

The phrase *the right place for the creative youth* follows *school,* the word modified.

PRACTICE

A *Read each sentence. Rewrite it, correcting the misplaced modifier. If there is no error, write **Correct.***

1. Ashley polished the cabinet that she had scratched.
2. Adrian, read *Robinson Crusoe*, a student.
3. The passenger tipped the taxi driver in evening clothes.
4. The cat purred at his owner with the fluffy tail.
5. Where are the fields that have recently been plowed?
6. You can achieve great things, who are young and ambitious.
7. The bike looked great to Erin, newly painted.
8. The clerk who sold the most goods got a raise.

B *Read the sentences. Rewrite them, correcting the misplaced modifiers.*

1. The hostess greeted me who wore a red dress.
2. Shaky and awkward, we saw the calf take its first steps.
3. Rover was very loyal to Laura, faithful and obedient.
4. The car was parked in front of the house with a convertible top.
5. Arranged on the table, the students sketched the fruits.
6. We could see the park sitting on the porch.
7. Hiding under his bed, Corey found his slippers.
8. We moved into the house on Central Street that we bought.

C *Read the paragraph. Rewrite it, correcting the 5 misplaced modifiers.*

A storm has been predicted by a reporter of hurricane force. He said that it could be the worst of the century with certainty. Meteorologists have been tracking the storm and its path at the National Weather Service. The eye is moving more quickly than anticipated by the reporter, at the center of the storm. As the storm moves toward land, the winds gather speed. As the reporter advised, we will take precautions, on TV.

> To avoid confusion, place modifiers as close as possible to the words they describe.

WRITE

Write a brief biographical sketch of someone you admire. The person may be someone you know personally or someone you have read about. Use modifiers correctly and effectively.

Writing Tip

Infinitives are verb forms that begin with *to*. When you write, do not **split infinitives** with modifiers.

Split: It is time **to** quietly **depart**.

Better: It is time **to depart** quietly.

You may sometimes split an infinitive, however, if you want to emphasize the modifier.

I am beginning **to** really **love** this!

SENTENCE FRAGMENTS

THINK ABOUT

A **sentence fragment** is a group of words that does not express a complete thought and cannot stand alone as a sentence.

Correct a sentence fragment by adding a missing *subject*, a missing *predicate*, or both.

Fragment: Dashed across the finish line.
Sentence: *The sprinters* dashed across the finish line.

Fragment: The difficult instructions.
Sentence: The difficult instructions *confused us.*

Fragment: Throughout her years in school.
Sentence: *Jamie made all As* throughout her years in school.

Correct a fragment in a piece of writing by joining it to a related sentence.

Fragment: During the break.
Sentence: The actor answered questions.
Joined: *The actor answered questions* during the break.

A *dependent clause* is a fragment because it does not express a complete thought; it cannot stand alone.

Dependent Clause: That I bought.
Sentence: *This is the game* that I bought.
Dependent Clause: When I'm tired.
Sentence: *I will rest* when I'm tired.

A *verbal phrase* is also a fragment because it does not express a complete thought; it cannot stand alone. (A verbal is a verb form used as a noun, an adjective, or an adverb. A *verbal phrase* is a verbal plus any related words.)

Verbal Phrase: Singing with the chorus.
Sentences: *I enjoy* singing with the chorus.
The girl singing with the chorus *is my sister.*

Verbal Phrase: Split by lightning.
Sentences: *The tree*, split by lightning, *died.*
Split by lightning, *the tree died.*

Verbal Phrase: To practice all day.
Sentences: *The players plan* to practice all day.
We like to practice all day.

STUDY A MODEL

Read the draft and the edit of a passage that a vacationer wrote.

draft: Back from my vacation. At Sara's Arizona home. Fantastic time! We went horseback riding every day. At sunset. Sara has a horse. Whom she named Sprite. During one ride. The horse galloped away. Almost throwing me!

edit: I am back from my vacation at Sara's Arizona home. I had a fantastic time! We went horseback riding every day at sunset. Sara has a horse whom she named Sprite. During one ride, the horse galloped away, almost throwing me!

Sentence fragments are red.

The draft is choppy and hard to read because of the many sentence fragments (*Back from my vacation, At Sara's Arizona home, Fantastic time,* for example).

Notice that the subject and verb *I am* have been added to the fragment *Back from my vacation.* Also, the fragment *At Sara's Arizona home* has been joined to the end of the sentence.

The dependent clause *Whom she named Sprite* has been joined to the independent clause *Sara has a horse.*

The verbal phrase *Almost throwing me* has been joined to the independent clause *The horse galloped away.*

PRACTICE

A *Combine the sentence fragment with the complete sentence. Add punctuation and joining words as needed.*

1. Keith keeps a diary. About his thoughts and experiences.
2. Everyone in my class went to the party. That Bryan gave.
3. Filling balloons with water. The children had fun.
4. From my bedroom window. I can see the park.
5. My faithful friend Alise. I trust.
6. Thomas resembles his father. Who is tall and dark.
7. Sitting in the first row. The man could clearly see the magician.
8. We flew the American flag. With great enthusiasm and pride.

B *Read each fragment. Add words to make it a complete sentence.*

1. Returned home after two days.
2. Often seen in nature magazines but rarely in the wild.
3. The digital camera from Photo World.
4. On a Saturday afternoon.
5. Before Thanksgiving vacation.
6. Surprised everyone.
7. Thomas Jones, my best friend.
8. Finding the door locked.

C *Read the following paragraph. Rewrite it, correcting the 8 fragments.*

Mahogany is a wood. That is frequently used for furniture making. Mahogany does not shrink or swell. Unless it is mistreated. Carpenters, who are fine furniture makers. Often select this wood. Mahogany is a handsome wood. Valued for its warm color. Mahogany has a color that sometimes changes. Growing darker in sunlight. Mahogany has a feathery pattern, or grain. If cut lengthwise. Mahogany is grown only in the tropics and must be imported. Makes it costly.

A **sentence fragment** is a group of words that does not express a complete thought and cannot stand alone as a sentence.

WRITE

Write a passage describing something you have seen in nature. Be sure to write complete sentences and avoid sentence fragments.

Writing Tip
In writing, remember to use **relative pronouns** (*who, whom, whose, which, that*) to begin **dependent clauses**.

   Dependent Clause: *that you remember*

Use **interrogative pronouns** (*who, whom, whose, which, what*) in **independent clauses** that are **questions**.

   Question : *What do you remember?*

35

THINK ABOUT

For variety in your writing, you can join two independent clauses to form *a compound sentence.*

My friend Anthony moved away. I miss him.
My friend Anthony moved away, **and** I miss him.

Sometimes you can also join two independent clauses to form a **complex sentence** by changing one of the independent clauses into a *dependent clause.*

To change independent clauses into dependent clauses, add **subordinating conjunctions,** which show various relationships between clauses.

Some subordinating conjunctions are: *after, although, as, as if, because, before, if, even if, since, so that, unless, until, when, whenever, where, wherever,* and *while.*

Here are four ways to form **complex sentences** using **subordinating conjunctions,** which show relationships.

You need help. I will assist. (simple sentences)
When you need help, I will assist. (time)
Wherever you need help, I will assist. (place)
If you need help, I will assist. (conditional)

You can also change an independent clause into a dependent clause by using **relative pronouns** (*who, whom, whose, which, what,* or *that*).

Remember to use a comma or commas to set off a dependent clause that is not essential to the meaning of the sentence.

Here are three ways to form **complex sentences** using **relative pronouns.**

The ambassador is my uncle. You met him once.
The ambassador, *whom* you met once, is my uncle.

I just read *Moby Dick.* It was written by Herman Melville.
I just read *Moby Dick, which* was written by Herman Melville.

The person is my friend Vera. She is waving.
The person *who* is waving is my friend Vera.

Here are the apples. I picked them.
Here are the apples *that* I picked.

STUDY A MODEL

Read this job performance evaluation. It contains several complex sentences.

Philip joined us last year, and he is a great asset to our firm. It has been five years **since** he became a registered architect. **While** he was still a student, he won several design contests. Philip decided on a career in architecture **because** he enjoys the creative aspects of design. Philip will remain in partnership with us **until** his assignments no longer challenge him. For now, he is an architect **who** meets every challenge. We will announce our opinion, **which** is unanimous. Philip will receive an immediate promotion.

Subordinating conjunctions are red, and relative pronouns are blue.

The first sentence is compound, containing two independent clauses joined by a comma and the conjunction *and.*

The second, third, fourth, and fifth sentences are complex and each contains a dependent clause that begins with a subordinating conjunction (*since, While, because, until*).

The sixth and seventh sentences are complex, containing the relative pronouns *who* and *which,* respectively.

The last sentence is a simple sentence.

PRACTICE

A *Read the sentences. Write the 4 subordinating conjunctions and the 3 relative pronouns.*

1. Bianca, who loves to act, is a colorful character.
2. Please read the manuscript that I completed today.
3. You should build a wall because you value your privacy.
4. Wherever the ground was moist, mushrooms sprouted.
5. The kittens took a nap after they had eaten.
6. The song, which I recorded last year, is on next.
7. We will hike on unless you are too fatigued.

B *Use each pair of independent clauses to form a complex sentence. Use the subordinating conjunction or relative pronoun in parentheses. Use commas correctly.*

1. Frieda wished for a pony. She was five. (when)
2. A tutor was hired. Lenny could do better in school. (so that)
3. The package arrived from Japan. Mom carefully opened it. (after)
4. The wheelchair ramp is helpful. Jeremy built it. (that)
5. The single eyewitness has not returned. She is our only hope. (who)
6. Your explanation is outrageous. It amused us. (which)
7. Kat often helps me with my homework. She has a lot of homework herself. (although)

C *Read the paragraph. Rewrite it by joining sentences that express related ideas. Form at least 1 compound sentence and 2 complex sentences.*

Frederick Law Olmsted was a landscape architect. He lived between 1822 and 1903. His contributions shaped urban landscapes. His contributions include more than 80 public parks. He took many trips to Europe. Olmsted was able to study European methods of landscape gardening. Olmsted planned New York's Central Park. His ideas were used for the preservation of Niagara Falls. He became the first commissioner of Yosemite National Park. He also designed the grounds for the Chicago World's Fair of 1893.

For sentence variety, you sometimes can join two independent clauses to form a **complex sentence** by changing one independent clause into a dependent clause, starting with either a **subordinating conjunction** or a **relative pronoun**.

WRITE

Write an evaluation of how you've progressed in a specific area of your life. The evaluation may relate to school, sports, hobbies, friends, or family. Use complex sentences to make your evaluation interesting.

Writing Tip
Remember to use a comma after an **introductory dependent clause**.

If you have time, please put up the birdhouse.

Although Sean was tired, he couldn't sleep.

Before you leave, give me a call.

JOINING SENTENCES WITH APPOSITIVES

THINK ABOUT

For sentence variety, you can sometimes join two related independent clauses by changing one clause to an appositive. An **appositive** is a word or a phrase that identifies or renames a noun or pronoun in the same sentence.

The cactus is a succulent. It stores water.
The cactus, *a succulent*, stores water.

Have you seen Al? Al is our blue parakeet.
Have you seen Al, *our blue parakeet*?

Today is June 21. It is my birthday.
Today is June 21, *my birthday*.

Eleanor Roosevelt was the wife of FDR.
Eleanor Roosevelt was an amazing woman.
Eleanor Roosevelt, *the wife of FDR*, was an amazing woman.

An appositive cannot stand alone as a sentence.
Incorrect: The blue SUV.
Correct: Our car, *the blue SUV,* needs gas.

Use a **comma or commas** with an appositive when the appositive is not essential; it could be removed without changing the meaning of the sentence.

My mother, *Edna*, was a big-band singer. (one mother only, so the name is not essential)
Henry Ford, *the inventor of the Model T,* made cars available to many Americans.
I take calcium, *an important mineral*.
Raul likes only one color, *blue*.

Do **not** use **a comma or commas** with an appositive that is essential to the noun or pronoun that it identifies or renames.

My friend *Ned* paints. (more than one friend)
Raul likes the color *blue*.
The mineral *calcium* comes in tablet form.

STUDY A MODEL

Read this description of Kahlil and Joline's adventure.

Kahlil and his friend Joline spotted an osprey, a type of hawk. Hawks are raptors, birds that eat other animals. The osprey, a fish eater, lives near water. On a high rock, Joline found the osprey's nest, a mass of intertwined sticks. Inside lay the osprey's precious possessions, four pale eggs. The guide, an ornithologist, cautioned Kahlil and Joline not to touch their discovery. He warned that the osprey might become aggressive. He was right! Diving and flapping, the osprey drove the intruders from her territory, the beach.

> *Appositives are red.*

Joline is an appositive renaming the noun *friend*. Notice that commas are not used with this appositive because it is needed in the sentence.

A fish eater is an appositive that explains or renames the *osprey*.

Commas are used around the appositive *an ornithologist,* which comes after the noun *guide* and renames it.

Don't confuse other kinds of modifiers with appositives. *Diving and flapping* are not appositives.

PRACTICE

A *Read the sentence. Write the appositive phrase and the word or words that it modifies. If there is no appositive phrase, write **No Phrase**.*

1. A seasoned camper, Joshua didn't mind being alone in the woods.
2. Her dress is periwinkle, a shade of blue.
3. My cousin Althea works downtown.
4. We were creeping along Interstate 45, the iciest road each winter.
5. They notified Mrs. Childress, the sheriff.
6. Although the water was cold, Stephie jumped in.
7. The concert will air on June 21, the summer solstice.
8. Because Richard loves tropical fruit, he chose the kumquat.

B *Join each pair of sentences by making the underlined words an appositive phrase. Use commas correctly.*

1. Becky dressed for the wedding. Becky was <u>the youngest bridesmaid</u>.
2. Eight o'clock came and went. It was <u>the hour of their arrival</u>.
3. The happiest person that night was Mr. Katz. Mr. Katz was <u>the chef</u>.
4. He remembers that adventure. It was <u>an archaeological dig</u>.
5. Marisa broke out in laughter. Marisa was <u>usually a serious person</u>.
6. Hail is <u>a type of freezing precipitation</u>. The hail bounced like golf balls.
7. Jasper decorates primarily with one color. The color is <u>red</u>.

C *Read the paragraph. Rewrite it by joining each pair of related sentences into a sentence that includes an appositive. Use commas correctly.*

Insects are arthropods. Arthropods are animals with bodies inside hard shells. An insect's body consists of three sections. The sections are the head, the thorax, and the abdomen. Insects touch, taste, and smell with their antennae. Antennae are delicate feelers on their heads. The thorax is the middle section of the body. The thorax contains the insect's legs and controls movement. The abdomen carries out functions related to digestion. The abdomen is the rear section.

> For sentence variety, you can sometimes join two related independent clauses by changing one clause to an appositive. An **appositive** is a word or phrase that identifies or renames a noun or pronoun in the same sentence.

WRITE

Write a description of a bird or an animal that you find interesting. Use appositives to add additional information to some of the sentences in your description.

Writing Tip
You can join related **simple sentences and complex sentences** by making one independent clause an appositive.

Simple: Jake is my cousin.

Complex: Jake wears safety glasses when he works.

Joined: Jake, my cousin, wears safety glasses when he works.

RUN-ON AND RAMBLING SENTENCES

THINK ABOUT

In your writing, avoid run-on sentences and rambling sentences because they confuse readers by running one idea into another. A **run-on sentence** has too many complete thoughts without correct punctuation. A **rambling sentence** has too many complete thoughts that are joined by conjunctions such as *and*, *but*, or *so*, without correct punctuation.

One way to correct a **run-on sentence** is to make **separate sentences** and use appropriate marks of punctuation: *periods, question marks,* or *exclamation points.*

Run-on Sentence: The question was vague, I could not answer it at the time.
Correct: The question was vague. I could not answer it at the time.

Run-on Sentence: Do you like opera I have always loved it.
Correct: Do you like opera? I have always loved it.

- Another way to correct a **run-on sentence** is to create a **compound sentence** by using a *comma* and a *coordinating conjunction* (*and, but, or*) or by using a *semicolon*.

  Run-on Sentence: We voted for the proposal, it was accepted by all the members.
  Correct: We voted for the proposal, **and** it was accepted by all the members.
  Correct: We voted for the proposal**;** it was accepted by all the members.

- Correct a **rambling sentence** by creating **separate sentences** (simple, compound, complex). Use appropriate connecting words and punctuation.

  Rambling Sentence: I bake bread at home and I sell most loaves in a bakery but I always keep a few for myself.
  Correct: I bake bread at home. I sell most loaves in a bakery. I always keep a few for myself. (3 simple sentences)
  Correct: I bake bread at home. I sell most loaves in a bakery, but I always keep a few for myself. (1 simple, 1 compound)
  Correct: I bake bread at home. Although I sell most loaves in a bakery, I always keep a few for myself. (1 simple, 1 complex)

STUDY A MODEL

Read the draft and edit of a theater company notice.

DIRECTOR

draft: Our theater company is performing a musical the director is Mr. Lemay. He was once a professional actor but eventually he retired and then he moved to our town. He arrived and we needed a director and Mr. Lemay volunteered. He got the job, we are pleased.

edit: Our theater company is performing a musical. The director is Mr. Lemay, who was once a professional actor. Eventually he retired and then moved to our town. When Mr. Lemay arrived, we needed a director. He volunteered, he got the job, and we are pleased!

In the draft, the first sentence is a run-on. In the edit, the first sentence has been split into two separate sentences with appropriate punctuation.

In the draft, the second sentence is rambling. It has three separate complete thoughts that run together with the conjunctions *but* and *and*. In the edit, the sentence has been broken into two separate sentences.

In the draft, the third sentence is rambling, and the fourth sentence is a run-on. In the edit, these sentences have been reworked into a complex sentence and a compound sentence.

PRACTICE

A *Use capital letters and correct punctuation to rewrite each run-on or rambling sentence.*

1. I loved the sci-fi film, Allan hated it!
2. Watch out there's a storm coming our way!
3. Pablo writes nonfiction articles he sells them to magazines.
4. You should disregard that notice, it is outdated.
5. I watch basketball on TV but my dad is a football fan and he enjoys the Super Bowl.

B *Rewrite each run-on sentence as a compound sentence, using the clue in parentheses. Rewrite each rambling sentence as two separate sentences with correct punctuation. Create at least one complex sentence.*

1. High winds accompanied the storm there were no torrential downpours. (comma + *but*)
2. A snake swallows its prey whole and a python can even swallow pigs and goats but it takes a long time to digest them.
3. Supermarkets reported slow sales last week department stores were practically empty. (comma + *and*)
4. Emily's new dress arrived yesterday and she tried it on instantly but it didn't fit and so it will have to be returned.
5. Boat owners sometimes add extra dock lines, they haul their boats from the water. (comma + *or*)
6. Skiers fled the avalanche zone flatter ground was safer. (semicolon)

C *Read the paragraph. Rewrite it by correcting any run-on or rambling sentences. Use appropriate capitalization, punctuation, and connecting words.*

A snake is an unusual animal it has many unique characteristics. To smell, the snake flicks its tongue in and out the tongue picks up odor particles. Then the snake places the particles against the roof of its mouth where there are nerve endings that connect to the smell center in the brain. Also, snakes have no eyelids and their eyes are always open and there are transparent shields over them. These reptiles once had limbs, their legs disappeared millions of years ago.

Correct **run-on sentences** or **rambling sentences** by creating separate sentences (simple, compound, complex). Include appropriate capitalization, punctuation, and connecting words.

WRITE

Write a notice for a musical or athletic event. Check your writing for any run-on or rambling sentences and then correct them.

Writing Tip
Avoid **comma splices,** or commas that incorrectly separate sentence parts.

Incorrect: Jan wrote the book, I read it.
Correct: Jan wrote the book; I read it.
Jan wrote the book, and I read it.

Incorrect: Erik ate, and then left.
Correct: Erik ate and then left.
Erik ate, and then he left.

REVISING SENTENCES

THINK ABOUT

Revise sentences to correct *structure* or *tense* or to delete *unnecessary* or *weak* words and phrases.

- For **parallel structure,** make sure two or more *similar* parts of a sentence are the same part of speech or have the same grammatical construction.

  Incorrect: Mia is a dancer, a singer, and *acts.*
  Correct: Mia is a dancer, a singer, and *an actress.*

  Incorrect: Roscoe spoke sincerely and *slow.*
  Correct: Roscoe spoke sincerely and *slowly.*

  Incorrect: Lee loves running and *to swim.*
  Correct: Lee loves running and *swimming.*
  Correct: Lee loves to run and *to swim.*

- Avoid **inconsistent verb tenses**. Don't shift from one tense to another unless the time of the action changes.

  Incorrect: The door *opens,* and Marit *entered.*
  Correct: The door *opens,* and Marit *enters.*
  Correct: The door *opened,* and Marit *entered.*
  Correct: The door *opened,* but Marit had already *entered.*

- Delete **unnecessary** or **weak** words, phrases, or clauses.

  Weak: *It is true that* a cactus holds water in its stem.
  Better: A cactus holds water in its stem.

  Weak: Caryn whispered her lines *softly.*
  Better: Caryn whispered her lines.

  Weak: He skimmed the *most* longest biography of *the life of* Jefferson.
  Better: He skimmed the longest biography of Jefferson.

  Weak: For this *here* recipe *you and I we* need boiling *hot* water.
  Better: For this recipe we need boiling water.

  Weak: *Like,* where is Lucas *at*?
  Better: Where is Lucas?

  Weak: *What I mean is,* I *totally* disagree.
  Better: I disagree.

  Weak: *You know,* the performance was *very* excellent.
  Better: The performance was excellent.

STUDY A MODEL

Read the draft and the edit of this theater review.

> **draft:** Last night's performance of the play, "In the Spotlight," was very predictable. In Act I, Michael, the main protagonist, finds that city life was interesting and a challenge. In Act II, Michael he is surprised to find that he likes being challenged and to live in the city.
>
> **edit:** Last night's performance of "In the Spotlight" was predictable. In Act I, Michael, the protagonist, finds that city life is interesting and challenging. In Act II, Michael is surprised to find that he likes being challenged and living in the city.

Faulty sentence structure is green, inconsistent verb tense is blue, and unnecessary words or phrases are red.

 The word *very* is unnecessary.

 The word *main* is unnecessary, since *protagonist* means "main character."

 The past-tense of *was* is inconsistent with *finds,* which is in the present tense.

 In the draft, *interesting* is an adjective, but *challenge* is a noun. The structure has been made parallel in the edit by replacing *challenge* with the adjective *challenging.*

 In the last sentence in the edit, *to live* has been replaced by *living,* making the structure parallel.

42

PRACTICE

A *Read each sentence. Rewrite it, eliminating any unnecessary words and phrases. If necessary, change capitalization or punctuation.*

1. As you know, Samantha and Iris they are best friends.
2. Because of the fact that school gets out at 3:15 P.M. in the afternoon, Joe can't be in the race.
3. Those twins they are the most smartest two people I know!
4. Without a sound, the cougar silently crossed the frozen ice field.
5. That there machine is a finely made, well-crafted piece of equipment.
6. The round sphere of the moon beamed through the darkness of night.

B *Read each sentence. Rewrite it, correcting faulty structure and inconsistent or incorrect verb tenses.*

1. Mr. Nadeau is a geologist, writer, and teaches.
2. Each year our class raises money and took a field trip.
3. Several hikers moved cautious and slowly along the ledge.
4. The plane flew low, and it passes right through the clouds.
5. The constellation had three bright stars that are forming a straight line.
6. These gymnasts like performing and to compete all year long.

C *Read the paragraph. Rewrite it, correcting errors in structure and verb tense. Delete any unnecessary words and phrases. Make other changes that will improve the text. For italics, use underlining.*

As you may or may not be aware, Mashid works for the *Clearwater News*, which was the local newspaper. Single-handedly, she alone covers the news events that occurred at night. She interviews eyewitnesses who have seen each event and will record their comments. Of course, she also takes notes, accurately and with quickness. After Mashid has collected the facts, she will return to the newspaper office. She is sitting down to her ten-year-old, practically ancient computer and thinks of a headline for the story. The headline must be descriptive but briefly. Mashid's editor likes reading and to edit Mashid's stories. Then the editor always approved her stories for publication.

Revise sentences to correct structure or verb tense and to delete unnecessary or weak words or phrases.

WRITE

Write a review of a movie you have seen. Read over your review and correct any errors you have made.

Writing Tip
Use the **active voice** to make your verbs more lively.
Passive: Those flowers were picked for me by Ana.
Active: Ana picked those flowers for me.
Passive: A tough game was won by our team.
Active: Our team won a tough game.

VARYING SENTENCES

THINK ABOUT

You can make your writing more effective by **varying sentences**. You can change the **structure**, the **length**, or the **type** of sentences that you use.

- Vary the **beginnings** of sentences by starting some sentences with a **modifier**.

    In the end, we all won.
    In defeat, the other team left the field.
    When the rain began, everyone ran for cover.
    With great speed, we ran for the tent.
    Looking proud, he stepped to the plate.
    Because she felt confident, she performed perfectly.

- For variety, sometimes change the normal **order of words** in a sentence, putting the verb before the subject.

    The enthusiastic *fans* **sat** in the stands.
    In the stands **sat** the enthusiastic *fans.*

    Our school *band* **is leading** the parade.
    Leading the parade **is** our school *band.*

- Vary the **length and type** of sentences. Use a combination of short and longer *simple, compound,* and *complex* sentences.

    Teddy Roosevelt loved nature. He helped establish many national parks. (simple sentences)
    Teddy Roosevelt loved nature, and he helped establish many national parks. (compound sentence)
    Because Teddy Roosevelt loved nature, he helped establish many national parks. (complex sentence)

- Create some sentences with *compound subjects* or *compound predicates.*

    We climbed Mount McVie. We then made camp.
    We climbed Mount McVie and then made camp. (simple sentence with compound predicate)

    Suki felt energetic. I felt energetic. We went for a hike.
    Suki and I felt energetic, and we went for a hike. (compound sentence; the first independent clause has a compound subject)

STUDY A MODEL

Read this description of a favorite pastime.

In the morning, Pam walks in the woods. She stops on her way and studies the many flowers along the path. Lady's slippers, with their elegant pink petals, are especially appealing. Because lady's slippers are scarce, Pam never picks them. Pam has a botanical notebook that she carries with her. When she sees a flower, she sketches it. Although Pam keeps it mainly as a scientific record, the book is almost a work of art. In it are her valuable sketches. This small book has become precious to Pam.

The first sentence is a simple sentence beginning with a prepositional phrase *(In the morning).*

The second sentence is a complex sentence; the independent clause has a compound predicate.

Notice that the fourth, sixth, and seventh sentences are complex sentences. They each begin with a clause.

The eighth sentence is in inverted order, with the verb *are* before the subject *sketches.*

In contrast to the longer surrounding sentences, the last sentence is a short simple sentence.

PRACTICE

A *Rewrite each sentence so that it begins with the underlined modifier. Use correct punctuation.*

1. An aide answered some questions <u>before the mayor appeared</u>.
2. The bus runs less frequently <u>during the summer months</u>.
3. Paul, <u>inspired by the exhibit</u>, enrolled in an art class.
4. This apartment complex was <u>originally</u> an old warehouse.
5. Kurt called ahead <u>since he was going to be late</u>.
6. The boisterous crowd <u>leaving the stadium</u> calmed down.
7. The designer drew a single line <u>expertly</u>.

B *Use the clues in parentheses to join each pair of sentences, making a compound or a complex sentence. Use correct punctuation.*

1. Yesterday there was little color on the ground. Today the shadows on the snow look blue. (compound; semicolon)
2. I won first prize. I had never expected it! (compound; *but*)
3. Jason's favorite sport was climbing trees. He was expert at it. (compound; *and*)
4. Mr. Stein has reference materials. They describe the mammals. (complex; *which*)
5. Elizabeth always returns things she borrows. She is conscientious. (complex; *who*)
6. This children's book includes illustrations. They are exceptionally beautiful. (complex; *that*)
7. Tami correctly pronounces scientific terms. She knows Latin. (complex; *who*)

C *Read the paragraph. Rewrite it, changing the type or length of some sentences. Add words, if necessary, and use correct punctuation.*

    Samuel Morse was quite versatile. He was an inventor. He was also an artist. Inventing occupied his time. Painting occupied his time. Morse made his living as an artist. He also entered art contests. Today he is not known as a portrait painter. He is not known as a founder of the National Academy of Design. The telegraph made Morse famous. He is mainly remembered as the inventor of the Morse Code.

Add variety to writing by changing the structure, length, or type of sentences.

WRITE

Write a description of your bedroom. Vary the structure, type, and length of sentences in your description.

Writing Tip

You can sometimes use **single words or phrases** or even short sentences for **emphasis** in your writing.

No! I will not go!
What? I don't believe it!
Brilliant!
What a world!
Good job!
Yes!

CAPITALIZATION: PEOPLE

THINK ABOUT

- **Capitalize** the **names** and **initials** of **specific people, animals,** and **fictional characters.**

  C. Lawrence Stein   Old Yeller
  E. V. McMurray   Spot
  Florence Nightingale   Scarlett O'Hara
  Elizabeth N. Anderson   E.T.

- Capitalize all **titles** and **abbreviated titles** used with names of people.

  Ms. Andrea Byrd   Detective Sly Gordon
  Sergeant Flynn   Harold Jay DeFazio, Sr.
  C. S. Juarez, M.D.   Emma Bartlett, Ph.D.
  Secretary Albright   President Lincoln
  Kate Reed, D.V.M.   Mrs. Ruth E. Thompson

  I took my cat *Annie* to *Sam Ritchie, D.V.M.*
  My friend *Bernice Clayton* likes the stories of *Edgar Allan Poe.*
  Sheila's advisor is *Morton Fisher, Ph.D.*
  My favorite character in *Johnny Tremain* is Paul Revere.

- Capitalize a **title** or a **family name** when it is used in place of a name or as part of a specific name.

  Wait for me, *Cousin*!
  Ask *Aunt Tracy* for the meat loaf recipe.
  Did *Mother* take the car today?
  May I help you, *Sir*?
  What is the assignment, *Professor*?

- Do not capitalize a title or a family name when it is not used to take the place of a name or when it is not used as part of a specific name.

  The *captain* took command.
  My *aunt* just bought a house.
  Will your *mom* come to the game?
  The *president* will contact you.

- Capitalize the names of **groups of people** from cities, states, regions, countries, and continents.

  Washingtonians   Southwesterners
  Hispanics   Australians

  New Yorkers and other *Northeasterners* stated their position.
  South Americans speak many languages.

STUDY A MODEL

Read this story of a family reunion.

> Our grandparents, parents, aunts, uncles, and cousins had gathered for a reunion. Even the dog Ruff was there. Few of us were native Kansans, but Aunt Gretchen and Grandma Pedersen had grown up nearby. We were amused when a passerby, Dr. Sven Wiborg, offered to take a family picture.
>
> "Madam," he said, "kindly stand next to your cousin."
>
> "Correction, Sir," Grandma replied, "that is not my cousin. That is Captain Olav T. Pedersen, Jr., and he is my husband!"

Specific names, titles, abbreviations, and groups are red.

In the first sentence, no titles are capitalized because they are not followed by names of specific people.

In the second sentence, *Kansans* is capitalized because it names a group of people from the state of Kansas. The titles *Aunt* and *Grandma* are capitalized because they are part of the names of specific people.

Notice that *Madam* and *Sir* are both capitalized because they are used here as names.

Captain Olav T. Pedersen, Jr. is capitalized because it is the name of a specific person. Notice that *husband* is not capitalized because it is not taking the place of a specific person.

PRACTICE

A *Write each item correctly. If there are no errors, write* **Correct.**

1. clark a. carlson
2. dr. d. l. groves
3. governor jesse winner
4. private barrows
5. michelle smart, d.d.s.
6. my cousin
7. martin c. riggoli, jr.
8. jill's grandmother
9. mary susan clemetti
10. sergeant sandi white
11. mr. and mrs. fujikawa
12. sen. william cohen
13. susan clare parker, ph.d.
14. mayor leland f. brown

B *Read the sentences. Find the 10 words or names that should be capitalized and write them correctly.*

1. I introduced dr. lily marlow to the students, most of whom were asians.
2. Will cousin harry meet my cousin in St. Paul?
3. "I can assure you, madam, that this is a fine garment," said the clerk.
4. You, auntie, have made me very happy.
5. Very quietly, mother said, "The phone call is from the doctor."
6. We heard gram talking to the postman, a fellow san franciscan.
7. The waiter told dad that the table was ready.
8. Sean extended his hand and said, "Hello, mayor."

C *Read the paragraph. Find the 10 words or names that should be capitalized and write them correctly.*

Cousin Stephen had an opportunity to work for senator theodore law before he was elected. Along with several other chicagoans, he prepared campaign literature to inform midwesterners about governor law and his running mate, general i. l. pease. While stephen was working, aunt stephanie encouraged me to join him. She said to me, "nephew, you should go visit your cousin. He could use some ideas from a californian."

When I asked father if I could go, he said, "Well, it might be a good experience."

Capitalize people's **names** and initials, titles, abbreviated titles, and words used as names. Also capitalize the names of groups of people from cities, states, regions, countries, and continents.

WRITE

Write a story in which characters from different places are introduced to one another at an event. Have the characters address each other by name and title. Capitalize names, titles, and group names correctly.

Writing Tip
When you write, remember to **capitalize proper adjectives**. These are adjectives that are formed from proper nouns.

I'll take *French* dressing.
Aaron's *Swiss* watch was a gift.
I'm interested in *Eastern* customs.
Louise prefers *Vermont* maple syrup.

CAPITALIZATION: PLACES

THINK ABOUT

- **Capitalize** the names of **specific places** such as *cities, districts, counties, states, provinces, regions, countries, continents,* and *planets.*

Cities:	Oregon City, Cairo
Districts:	Fifth Congressional District, District of Columbia
Counties:	Orange County, County Cork
States:	Missouri, Nevada
Provinces:	Alberta, Nova Scotia
Regions:	the Midwest, the Northwest
Countries:	Poland, Venezuela
Continents:	North America, Asia
Planets:	Jupiter, Venus

- Capitalize **directional words** when they name regions. Do not capitalize these words when they give directions.

  Landforms in the *West* are dramatic. (region)
  Leonard walked *west* for a mile. (direction)
  Samantha felt at home in the *Southeast*. (region)
  The tourists drove *southeast* of town. (direction)

- **Capitalize** the names of **specific places** such as *mountains, parks, beaches, bodies of water, islands, landmarks/monuments/public areas, landforms, buildings, bridges,* and *roadways.*

Mountains:	Mt. St. Helens, Mauna Loa
Parks:	Acadia National Park, Central Park
Beaches:	Ipanema Beach, Old Orchard Beach
Bodies of Water:	Klickitat River, Indian Ocean, Great Salt Lake
Islands:	Monhegan Island, Aleutian Islands
Landmarks, Monuments, Public Areas:	Plymouth Rock, Vietnam Veterans Memorial, Stonehenge
Landforms:	Cumberland Gap, Angel Falls
Buildings:	Empire State Building, Taj Mahal
Bridges:	Bridge of Sighs, Old London Bridge
Roadways:	Route 66, Los Angeles Freeway, Maple Street

STUDY A MODEL

Read this description of of a trip that Ken took.

Ken lives in Honolulu on the island of Oahu in the state of Hawaii. Ken's family took a trip to visit relatives in California. In San Francisco, they visited Ghirardelli Square and the Golden Gate Bridge. They saw Stinson Beach and Muir Woods and then traveled north on Interstate 5. They had a wonderful visit, but Ken won't mind returning to his own home to see Waikiki Beach, the majestic peak of Diamond Head, and the many other captivating sights.

> *Specific place names are red.*

Honolulu is capitalized because it is the name of a specific city; *Oahu* is the name of a specific island; and *Hawaii* is the name of a specific state.

Golden Gate Bridge, Stinson Beach, and *Muir Woods* are capitalized because they name a specific bridge, beach, and public area, respectively.

The word *north* is not capitalized because it names a direction, not a region. The word *peak* is not capitalized because it does not name a specific place.

Waikiki Beach and *Diamond Head* are capitalized because they do name specific places.

PRACTICE

A *Read the phrases. Write the names of the specific places correctly.*

1. admiring montreal
2. from south korea
3. the countries of asia
4. in westchester county
5. enjoying oliver beach
6. penguins in antarctica
7. studying the west
8. visiting washington
9. observing venus
10. entering new brunswick
11. a rock from montana
12. rings of saturn

B *Read the sentences. Find the names of the 12 specific places that should be capitalized and write them correctly.*

1. In the northeast, the sun often shines after a big snowfall.
2. Ms. Leland showed us slides of the grand coulee dam.
3. Kendall brought in snapshots of the rocky mountains and spruce knob in west virginia.
4. The northern part of minnesota is famous for boundary waters canoe area wilderness.
5. I felt far from my home near times square in new york city.
6. Marta hiked along the sakatah singing hills state trail.
7. They crossed the continental divide on the way to carlsbad caverns.

C *Read the paragraphs. Find and correct the 17 names of specific places that should be capitalized.*

Think about all the scenic vistas there are to see. In north america alone, one can travel from cities such as vancouver, british columbia, to new orleans, louisiana. Imagine canoeing to isle royale in lake superior or hiking near mt. mckinley in alaska.

Every region in the united states has its own appeal. You can travel major highways, such as the pan american highway, or legendary ones, such as route 66. The east alone offers coasts, mountains, and coastal plains. Then there are the wondrous landscapes of the south, the north, the west, and the midwest. The options for travel are endless.

Capitalize the names of **specific places**, and capitalize **directional words** when they name regions.

WRITE

Write a description of an area, close to home or far away, that would be interesting to tourists. Identify its location. Then give the names of specific places that the visitors might enjoy seeing. Be sure to use capitalization correctly.

Writing Tips

- Unless the article **the** begins a sentence, do not capitalize **the** with a **place name**.
   We visited **the Gulf.**
   The Gulf was beautiful.
- Capitalize the word **earth** when it is used with the names of other planets but not when it is not used as the name of a planet or when it is preceded by the article **the**.
   We studied Mars, Venus, and **Earth.**
   That is the oldest tree on **earth.**
   The **earth** is home to many species.

CAPITALIZATION: THINGS

THINK ABOUT

Capitalize the names of most **specific things**. Do not capitalize the names of general things.

- Capitalize the names of **months, days, holidays, special events,** and **historical periods**.

Month:	September
Day:	Wednesday
Holiday:	Thanksgiving
Special Event:	New Year's Eve
Historical Event:	World War II
Historical Period:	the Renaissance

- Capitalize the names of specific **forms of transportation**, including *ships, railroads, airlines,* and *spacecraft*.

Ship:	H.M.S. *Titanic*
Railway:	Tioga Central
Airline:	Aloft
Spacecraft:	*Apollo 13*

- Capitalize **brand names** of products (but not types of products).

Soft Drink:	Thirst-O
Tool:	Hefty Turn wrench

- Capitalize the names of **groups**, including *government groups, companies, organizations, clubs,* and *teams*.

Government Group:	Department of the Interior
Company:	The Main Stay
Organization:	Cub Scouts of America
Club:	Sierra Club
Team:	Who-Needs-Luck

- Capitalize the names of **languages, races, nationalities,** and **religions**.

Language: Spanish		**Race:** Asian	
Nationality: Italian		**Religion:** Buddhism	

- Capitalize in **titles** the first word, last word, and each important word (articles, short conjunctions, and short prepositions are not capitalized unless they are the first or last word).

  Poem: "Tall Grass" **Essay:** "My Name"
  Article: "The Challenge of Skateboarding"
  Short Story: "The Fall of the House of Usher"
  Document: Declaration of Independence
  Magazine: *National Geographic World*
  Book: *Sea Wolf* **Film:** *Black Beauty*
  Newspaper: *Patriot Ledger Times*
  Song: "America the Beautiful"
  Play: *Tim* **Painting:** *Fog Warning*
  Long Musical Work: *William Tell Overture*

STUDY A MODEL

Read the paragraph about two friends, Ty and Jack.

Ty and Jack met at Central College on Halloween, the fourth Friday of their freshman year. During a ride to school on the Green Line subway, they shared a box of Betty's Best blueberry muffins and compared goals. Jack's favorite book was Designing Electric Cars. He wanted to work for Carcraft Motors Company. Ty was in the Astronomy Club, and he wanted to work at Spacecraft Unlimited. They met in the fall, five years later. Jack was working for the State Department of Transportation and Ty was working for Sky Rover.

> *Names of specific things are red.*

Central College is capitalized because it is the name of a specific institution.

Halloween and *Friday* are capitalized because they name a specific special day and a specific day of the week. However, *freshman year* is not capitalized, because it names a general period of time. *Green Line* is capitalized because it is the name of a subway line, but the word *subway* is not capitalized because it is not part of the name of the company.

State Department of Transportation is the name of a government group, and *Sky Rover* is the name of an airline.

PRACTICE

A *Read each title. Rewrite it, capitalizing words correctly. Use underlining for italics.*

1. "songs of seals, wails of whales" (poem)
2. *life on the river; home in the mountains* (book)
3. *collectors of rocks weekly newsmagazine* (news magazine)
4. *the views of mount denali* (story)
5. declaration for peace, harmony, and justice (document)
6. *san francisco daily news* (newspaper)
7. "a report on hawaii's volcanoes" (report)

B *Read the sentences. Find the 8 names of specific things that should be capitalized and write the names correctly. Use underlining for italics.*

1. To get inland, Consuelo got tickets on cloud airways.
2. Madame LeCren taught me to speak french.
3. The inflatable raft *wave rider* carried sightseers along the remote coast.
4. Jan Vermeer's *portrait of a woman* is a painting that seems to glow.
5. On the monitor, they could watch the space station, *mir*.
6. "In my opinion," she whispered, "*the canterbury tales* is the great masterpiece of the middle ages!"
7. Mike drove Addie down the boulevard in his turquoise and black 1964 chevy convertible.

C *Read the paragraph. Find the 7 names of specific things that should be capitalized and write them correctly. Use underlining for italics.*

Owen's sister Rhian graduated from gerard university, spoke French well, drank stargazer's coffee, and could play "greensleeves" on the piano. Although the league of women voters had held a debate in april, she had not attended. Instead she had chosen to view a new film at the malimax theater. This decision was considered unacceptable by her aunt, Ms. D. O. Welle, who was campaigning for a seat in the senate. Ms. Welle reprimanded her, but Rhian defended her choice.

Capitalize the names of most **specific things**.

WRITE

Write a paragraph about you and a friend. Include the names of some specific things in your paragraph.

Writing Tips
- Capitalize **school subjects** only when they are languages or course names.
  Lamar took a *biology* class. (subject)
  Lamar took a *French* class. (language)
  Do you like *History 2*? (course name)
- Do not capitalize the names of **seasons** unless they are part of a name.
  I like *spring*. I went to the *Spring Fling*.

THINK ABOUT

Using **commas** to set off various items makes your writing easier to read.

- Use a *comma* after the **greeting** in a friendly letter and after the **closing** in any letter.
  Dear Uncle Phillip, (greeting)
  Sincerely, (closing)

- Use a *comma* to separate items in **dates** and **addresses**. In a date, place a comma between the day and the year. In a sentence, add another comma after the year. In an address, place a comma between the city and state. In a sentence, add another comma after the state.
  May 4, 1984   On May 4, 1984, Jim was born.
  Austin, Texas   Austin, Texas, is their hometown.

- Use a *comma* to set off an **introductory word** such as *yes, no, why, sure,* or *well.*
  Yes, this apple is perfectly crisp! Sure, I'll go.

- Use a *comma* to set off a **noun of direct address**.
  Leanne, where is your jacket?
  I left it at the hockey game, Mother!
  It's time, Spencer, to go to bed.

- Use *commas* to set off a **parenthetical expression**, which interrupts a sentence.
  Of course, we're going to be very late!
  The proof, I believe, is faulty.
  The conclusion is true, nevertheless.

- Use *commas* to separate two or more **adjectives** that equally modify the same **noun**.
  This hot, humid weather will end soon.

- Use a *comma* to set off a **long phrase** or **clause** at the beginning of a sentence.
  Sorting all the linens, Elena found her ring.
  With fame in mind, Conrad signed his sketch.
  Although junk food is tempting, I rarely eat it.

- Remember to use *commas* to set off a **phrase** or a **clause** that is *not essential*; it could be removed without changing the basic meaning of the sentence.
  Wuthering Heights, my favorite book, is out.
  The traveler, *exhausted from the trip,* fell asleep.
  Roberto, *who is very kind,* joined in.

- Do *not* use *commas* to set off a phrase or clause that is *essential* to the basic meaning of the sentence.
  The car *that they want* is red.
  I prefer the color *blue.*

STUDY A MODEL

Read the letter from Stephanie to her pen pal, Huang.

> 125 North Street
> Cheyenne, Wyoming 82001
> September 5, 2005
>
> Dear Huang,
>   Yes, we drove across the country to Boston, Massachusetts, last month. My brother, who had always wanted to live in the East, moved to Boston on August 15, 2001, and we went to visit him. When we arrived in Boston, my brother took us to Brookline, Massachusetts, the birthplace of John F. Kennedy. Seeing this cosmopolitan, lively town was a treat.
>   Your friend, Stephanie

Commas are red.

The return address includes a comma between the city and the state. The date includes a comma after the day of the month.

Since this is a friendly letter, both the greeting and the closing are followed by commas. If it were a business letter, the greeting would be followed by a colon.

Within the second sentence of the first paragraph, commas go before and after the year. Because the clause *who had always wanted to live in the East* is not essential to the basic meaning of the sentence, it is set off by commas.

In the last sentence, a comma separates two adjectives that equally modify the noun *town.*

PRACTICE

A *Rewrite each item, placing commas correctly.*

1. Dear Mom and Dad
2. Yours truly
3. July 4 1776
4. Saratoga Springs New York
5. Dear Aunt Molly
6. San Luis Obispo California
7. August 20 2000
8. Your cousin
9. New Year's Day 2003
10. Dear Arlen and Eva
11. Cordially yours
12. February 1 1990
13. Great Falls Montana
14. Dear Miss Hendricks

B *Read each sentence. Rewrite it, adding commas as needed.*

1. According to science we are surrounded by an infinite variety of colors.
2. You have experienced similar events in your lifetime I am sure.
3. To tell the truth our eyes constantly trick us.
4. The polar bear's long thick heavy fur keeps it warm in the Arctic.
5. Desert lizards with their compact leathery bodies can endure long hot dry days in the desert.
6. His long wavy black hair shone in the sun.
7. Oh what a splendid sunrise!
8. Here they are now Mrs. Yee with a new spotlight.

C *Read the paragraph. Rewrite it, adding 10 commas where they are needed.*

Jane Austen who lived from 1775 to 1817 was a novelist. She lived in Hampshire a county in central England. She wrote amusing novels about people some of whose behavior she considered silly. Known as comedies of manners Austen's novels depict her familiar world. Austen who acknowledged her authorship only to her nearest dearest friends received little public recognition while she was alive. This in my opinion is not surprising. None of her books published during her lifetime bore her name. The people about whom she wrote never knew her as an author.

Use **commas** to separate or set off various elements to make your writing easier to understand.

WRITE

Write a letter to a friend in which you describe a recent event that took place in your school or your neighborhood. Include a return address, date, greeting, and closing. Throughout your letter, use commas correctly.

Writing Tip

To decide whether **adjectives** modify a noun equally, try this trick.

Mentally insert the word *and* between the adjectives. If the sentence reads well, use a comma when *and* is omitted.

She gave a witty, informative speech.
(She gave a witty and informative speech.)

Lucy ate a spicy Italian sausage.
(Lucy ate a spicy and Italian sausage.)

THINK ABOUT

- Use an **apostrophe** to replace the omitted letter or letters in a **contraction**. Here are some examples.

isn't *(is + not)*   you'd *(you + had or would)*
didn't *(did + not)*   he's *(he + is)*
don't *(do + not)*   who's *(who + is)*
weren't *(were + not)*   what's *(what + is)*
can't *(can + not)*   they're *(they + are)*
I'd *(I + had or would)*   they've *(they + have)*
she'd *(she + had or would)*   we'll *(we + will)*

He *did not* see me. He *didn't* see me.
They have left for school. *They've* left for school.

- Use an **apostrophe** to replace the omitted numbers in a **date**.

'85 (1985)   They met in *'85*.

- The possessive form of nouns or pronouns shows **ownership**. Use an **apostrophe and s ('s)** to make the possessive form of a singular noun.

the *worker's* tools   one *deer's* tracks

- Use an **apostrophe and s ('s)** to make the possessive form of a plural noun that does not end in *s*.

four *deer's* tracks   the *oxen's* yokes

- Use only an **apostrophe (')** to make the possessive form of a plural noun that ends in *s*.

three *friends'* home   two *artists'* brushes

- Use an **apostrophe and s ('s)** to form the possessive of a **compound noun** or an **indefinite pronoun**.

My *mother-in-law's* letters are written on her finest stationery. (compound noun)
One's attitude is very important.
(indefinite pronoun)

Remember that a possessive pronoun does not include an apostrophe.

Which hat is *hers*? (not *her's*)
Its fur is very silky.

- To form the possessive of **two or more nouns** that share ownership of something, add an **apostrophe and s ('s)** to the last noun.

We went to *Lacy, Rob, and Pia's* house.
The *dog and cat's* game lasted all morning.

STUDY A MODEL

Read this stand-up comic's jokes.

Why didn't the officers take the call?
    It was only a bird's call.
How did 2000 get ahead of '99?
    It was a leap year.
How will we know when Ann and Andy's train arrives?
    We'll keep track of it.
Why aren't both countries' ships floating in the ocean?
    They're floating in space.
    They're spaceships.
What's a good name for your sister-in-law's family?
    Your outlaws.

Apostrophes are red.

Didn't, We'll, aren't, They're, and *What's* are contractions.
Bird's is the possessive form of a singular noun.
The date *'99* uses an apostrophe in place of omitted numbers.
Ann and Andy's is the shared possessive form of two proper nouns.

Countries' is the possessive form of a plural noun.

Sister-in-law's uses *'s* to make the possessive form of a compound noun.

PRACTICE

A *Read each phrase. Write the possessive form of the underlined noun.*

1. the <u>announcer</u> voice
2. some <u>men</u> suits
3. the <u>commander-in-chief</u> pen
4. the <u>mice</u> cheese
5. most <u>kangaroos</u> pouches
6. the <u>geese</u> feathers
7. <u>women</u> skin
8. those <u>voters</u> ballots
9. one <u>rancher</u> cattle
10. the many <u>immigrant</u> hopes
11. the <u>manager</u> duties
12. <u>Mark</u> composition
13. my <u>brother-in-law</u> house
14. his favorite <u>Teddy bears</u> cap

B *Read the sentences. Write the 9 underlined possessives, contractions, and dates correctly.*

1. Our English <u>teachers</u> handwriting is almost always legible.
2. My problem <u>wasnt</u> the same as <u>her's</u>.
3. <u>Whos</u> going to be the first to volunteer?
4. By <u>86</u> <u>theyd</u> begun to notice that the decade was half over.
5. The <u>secretary-generals</u> duties are a mystery.
6. <u>Sal and Mandys</u> partnership is off to a good start.
7. Those <u>childrens</u> books are beautifully illustrated.

C *Read the paragraph. Rewrite it, correcting the 7 errors in apostrophe use.*

Recently our math club read the article, "Its Time to Calculate the Rate of Expansion." This work, written in the summer of 99, raised some questions. The author stated that certain scientists theories argue that the universe is expanding. Five peoples contradictory reports were quoted throughout the article. However, our math teachers questions werent fully answered. Our logical conclusion is that youve got to be meticulously precise and thorough when you write a scholarly article.

Use **apostrophes** in **contractions**, in place of **omitted numbers in dates**, and to form **possessives**.

WRITE

Write a humorous story about a family that has too many possessions. Include possessives, contractions, and at least one shortened form of a year. Use apostrophes correctly.

Writing Tip

When **ownership** is separate, each name should show possession.

Marlee's and Phil's reports are finished. (Marlee and Phil each have a report.)

Marlee and Phil's report is finished. (The one report belongs to both Marlee and Phil.)

THINK ABOUT

Use **quotation marks** to set off **direct quotations,** the exact words of a speaker.

- Use a **punctuation mark** after the last word of a direct quotation. This mark should be a **comma** when the quotation comes first in the sentence and is a statement or command. This mark should be a **period** when the quotation comes last in the sentence and is a statement or a command. Always place a **comma** or a **period** *before* the quotation mark.

    "This book is my favorite," Julio declared.
    Julia said, "Look at this one."

- Place a **question mark** or an **exclamation point** *before* the quotation mark if the quotation itself is a question or exclamation. Otherwise, place the punctuation mark *after* the quotation mark.

    "Where's my canary?" asked Reiko.
    Did I hear you say, "Let's eat"?
    I couldn't believe it when he said, "You won"!

- In an **interrupted quotation**, an explanatory speaker tag "interrupts" the quotation. Use **commas** to set off the *speaker tag*.

    "That bird," said Kay, "is an oriole."

- Do not use quotation marks to set off *indirect quotations*, which tell what someone said without using exact words.

    Cleo said she'd go. Cleo said, "I'll go."

- Use **quotation marks** only at the beginning and at the end of a quotation of two or more sentences.

    "I know it's late. I'm not at fault. See what happened?" said Janna, pointing to her flat tire.

- A **dialogue** is a conversation that contains direct quotations. When you write dialogue, start a new paragraph for each speaker. Remember to indent.

    "Wait for me!" yelled Ernie as he chased after his older brother, Bobby.
    "Hurry up, Ern," urged Bobby.

- Use **quotation marks** before and after **titles** of *stories, poems, articles, chapters, radio and TV programs*, and *songs*.

    "Godmother" (story), "Nova" (TV program)

- Use **italics** (when using a computer) or **underlining** (when writing by hand) with the titles of longer works such as *books, magazines, newspapers, movies, plays*, and *CDs*.

    Child of the Owl (book), *Teen Ink* (magazine), *Death of a Salesman* (play)

- Use **quotation marks** to set off *special words and phrases*.

    The envelope was marked "Private."

STUDY A MODEL

Read this story dialogue, which contains direct quotations.

As they walked, Gwyn confided to Terry, "Liz's feelings are hurt because we haven't invited her."

"How do you know?" Terry asked.

"Well," Gwyn explained, "she was singing a line from a song that has to do with feeling left out."

Terry said, "Are you sure that means her feelings are hurt?"

"Wouldn't your feelings be hurt if you felt left out? Mine would," Gwyn reasoned.

"Then there's only one thing to do," Terry said. "What's her number? Let's pick up the phone and call her now!"

Quotation marks are red.

In the first and second sentences, quotation marks set off direct quotations in the dialogue. Notice the new indented paragraph for a change of speaker.

The third paragraph includes an interrupted quotation. Quotation marks set off the two parts of the interrupted quotation. Notice that the first word in the second part of the quotation (*she*) begins with a small letter.

In the last paragraph, quotation marks are used only at the beginning and end of the quotation, which is more than one sentence long.

PRACTICE

A *Read each sentence. Add end punctuation and quotation marks for each underlined word.*

1. Joshua said, "Let's go to the <u>beach</u>
2. Ginger just said to me, "I can't come with <u>you</u>
3. Don't ever say, "I <u>quit</u>
4. Mom yelled, "Turn that radio <u>down</u>
5. Marie exclaimed, "I love that <u>cake</u>
6. Did Kristal say, "We should thank <u>them</u>
7. "I'll be home on Sunday," Ray said, "but don't tell <u>Dad</u>

B *Read each item. Rewrite it, adding correct punctuation. If there are no errors, write* **Correct.**

1. Grandpa said that he watched the TV show "Howdy Doody" as a kid.
2. I don't know much about her skills. Can you tell me what else she's done? I'm very interested Susan's new teacher said.
3. Those are major accomplishments! Arthur exclaimed. I didn't know a single inventor could make so many things. When did he live?
4. What did he mean by that remark? questioned Rosalie.
5. Uncle Jeff said, I can't get the song Casey Jones out of my mind!

C *Read this dialogue. Rewrite it, adding quotation marks and indents as needed.*

Where are you going with Chico? asked Inez. I already walked him this morning.

Mom told me to take Chico for a walk, explained José. I told her that you had already walked Chico this morning, but she insisted.

Inez said, That's odd. Mom isn't usually like that. Was she angry about something else?

I don't think so, said José.

Then they heard their mother say, This puppy is driving me crazy!

Oh, no, José said, it looks like Chico chewed the strap on Mom's purse.

Look at Chico, Inez said. He looks guilty!

Use **quotation marks** to set off **direct quotations, special words,** and some **titles.** Use **italics** or underlining for **titles** of books, magazines, newspapers, movies, plays, and CDs.

WRITE

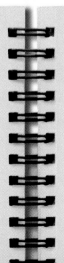

Write a short story in which the characters reveal their personalities through dialogue. Use quotation marks and other punctuation correctly.

Writing Tip
• Using **single quotation marks** to set off a **quotation within a quotation.**

   "Father shouted, 'Be quiet!' to everyone in the library," Krista said.

   James told Dan, "Coach Rizzo said, 'We'll win this one.' "

THINK ABOUT

A **paragraph** is a group of sentences about a single idea. A paragraph consists of a **topic sentence** and supporting **detail sentences**. Always **indent** the first word of a paragraph.

A **topic sentence** states the **main idea** of a paragraph. The topic sentence may be anywhere in a paragraph, but it is usually at the beginning or at the end.

Main Idea: Desert landscapes differ.
Deserts differ from one another in many ways. Some deserts consist of drifting sand dunes. Others consist of hard-packed clay or rock. Deserts may be large or small, hilly or flat. They may be located below sea level or on high plateaus. Deserts have various characteristics.

Main Idea: All deserts are dry.
In all deserts, there is very little rainfall. Both the earth and the air are dry. Desert plants and animals manage to survive without a regular source of water. *One thing that all deserts have in common is dryness.*

The other sentences in a paragraph are called **detail sentences**. These sentences develop the main idea with *facts, examples,* or *opinions.*

Fact: Dog breeds came into existence 3,000 to 4,000 years ago.

Example: One type of dog entered in national dog shows is the Border collie.

Opinion: Beagles make the best pets.

Detail sentences may also use *sensory words,* or words related to the five senses (sight, sound, smell, taste, touch), to create vivid mental images for readers.

Sensory Detail: My dog's bark is so loud and sharp that people two blocks away can hear him.

STUDY A MODEL

Read this writer's impression of Bleecker Street on summer afternoons.

On humid August afternoons, Bleecker Street was a kaleidoscope of smells, sounds, sights, and sensations. The aromas of hot pizza and roasted peanuts mingled with the choking exhaust of passing buses, cabs, and automobiles. Honking horns and the piercing shouts of excited children filled the air. Beneath frayed green awnings, short and shabby shops stood squeezed into a row of red brick buildings. This was Bleecker Street.

Sensory details are red.

The main idea of the paragraph is Bleecker Street in August.

The first sentence of the paragraph is the *topic sentence*. It presents Bleecker Street as an intense sensory experience on August afternoons.

The detail sentences develop the topic sentence by giving several examples of experiences on Bleecker Street on August afternoons. The details also include sensory words to create vivid mental images for readers.

PRACTICE

A *Read each detail sentence. Write* **Fact, Example,** *or* **Opinion** *to tell the type of details used.*

1. The cheeses included Edam from Holland and provolone from Italy.
2. The Vikings built the best ships in the world.
3. Spiders have eight legs, but insects have only six legs.
4. One type of quilt has patterns made up of squares and triangles.
5. Chocolate is made from the seeds of the cacao tree.
6. Bigfoot and the Yeti are real.

B *Match each main idea with the detail sentence that develops it.*

Main Ideas

1. Some folk songs are humorous.
2. Folk music is influenced by diverse cultures.
3. The writers of many folk songs are unknown.

Detail Sentences

a. Nobody knows who wrote the Scottish love song "Loch Lomond."
b. "My Darling Clementine" is a funny ballad about a gold miner's daughter.
c. American spirituals reflect both African and European influences.

C *Read the underlined topic sentence and the 8 detail sentences. Of the detail sentences, 5 clearly support the topic sentence. Write a paragraph using the topic sentence and the 5 detail sentences.*

<u>Iceland proved to be a good place for Norwegians in need of new land to settle.</u>

1. The island had a weird, barren beauty.
2. On the coasts were rich grazing lands for cattle.
3. Inland were heaths suitable for sheep grazing.
4. The rivers were full of trout and salmon.
5. In winter the sea was cold and dangerous.
6. The seas could be fished for cod and herring.
7. Little of the land was suitable for farming.
8. The Gulf Stream kept the climate from being too cold.

A **paragraph** is a group of sentences about one main idea. The **topic sentence** of a paragraph states the **main idea**, and **detail sentences** develop it.

WRITE

Write a paragraph describing a place you know very well. Write a clear topic sentence and include facts and examples to develop the main idea. Also add sensory language to create a strong mental image of the place for readers. Remember to indent.

Writing Tips
- Remember to **conclude** a paragraph with a sentence that signals readers that the idea is complete.
- The following types of writing all consist of paragraphs with main ideas and supporting details:
  descriptive (descriptions), **narrative** (real or imaginary stories), **expository** (information, explanations), and **persuasive** (opinions).

PARAGRAPHS: LEADS AND TRANSITIONS

THINK ABOUT

A strong **lead** and effective **transitional words** help you gain and hold your reader's attention.

- A **lead** is one or two sentences that lead into the rest of a paragraph. The lead might be a startling *question*, a surprising *statement of fact*, an intriguing *quotation*, or a fascinating *description*.

> Have you ever dreamed of flying? If so, you are not alone. (question)

> One plus one does not invariably equal two. (surprising statement)

> "It is a fine thing to be honest, but it is also very important to be right," Winston Churchill once observed. (quotation)

> On the night that Alexa crossed the border, she had no idea how much her life was about to change. The lights ahead shone ominously, and Alexa shuddered instinctively. (description)

- **Transitional words or phrases** help to link ideas between sentences and paragraphs. The following are various kinds of transitional words.

  location: above, below, behind, beside, against, in front, before, to the right, on the left, in the middle, opposite, toward, underneath

  time: first, next, last, before, during, after, while, meanwhile, soon, eventually, finally, once, sometimes, occasionally, never, later, recently, today, at the present time, in the future, at the same time, to begin with

  emphasis: in fact, indeed, regardless, nevertheless

  example: for example, such as, for instance, including, additionally, furthermore

  conclusion or summary: in conclusion, in summary, in other words

  comparison (similarity): as, just as, like, likewise, similarly

  contrast (difference): but, however, yet, unlike, although, on the other hand, in contrast, conversely

  cause/effect: because, therefore, since, consequently, as a result, thus, so

STUDY A MODEL

Read this paragraph about a mysterious discovery.

In the town archives, someone discovered pages from an antique manuscript. Many pages were torn, and few were easy to read. Although some archivists speculated that the manuscript was an almanac, others thought it was a ship captain's diary from centuries ago. Eventually, several experts were consulted. After analyzing the paper, the handwriting, and the language of the document, one announced, "This is the first weather forecast ever discovered in the United States." Finally the mystery was solved.

The lead is red, and the transitional words are blue.

> The lead will arouse readers' curiosity about the content of the manuscript.

> The transitional word *Although* introduces a contrast between the archivists' ideas.

> The transitional words *Eventually, After,* and *Finally* all indicate the time when various events took place.

PRACTICE

A *Read each sentence. Write the transitional word or phrase.*

1. In conclusion, the author refuses to be interviewed.
2. The determined group persevered nevertheless.
3. Likewise, I am inclined to agree.
4. As many birds do, squirrels make their nests in trees.
5. By contrast, some protesters insisted that diplomacy was the answer.
6. Consequently, the most articulate contestants won the prize.
7. As a result, the argument still holds.
8. At the present time, I have no suggestions.

B *Complete each sentence by writing one of the following transitional words or phrases:* **recently, because, however, eventually, while, additionally.**

1. He makes a few persuasive points; ____, most of his logic is faulty.
2. ____ she thought she had no alternative, Eliza sold flowers.
3. ____ I will have to do my homework.
4. ____, I offer the following pieces of evidence.
5. ____ Nero fiddled, the city burned.
6. ____ I've realized how fortunate I am.

C *Read the paragraph. Rewrite it, using a strong lead and transitional words to link the ideas in the sentences.*

Rainwater does not last in the desert. The rain falls. Bright sunshine appears. The rain quickly evaporates. The floors of some deserts are covered with loose sand or rock. The rain sinks rapidly through it. Other desert floors are hard-packed earth. In this type of desert, the rainwater runs off into gulleys where it seeps under the surface.

A **lead** is one or two sentences that lead into the rest of a paragraph. **Transitional words** help to link ideas between the sentences in a paragraph.

WRITE

Write a paragraph about a discovery. Make sure the lead and transitional words are strong enough to capture and hold readers' interest.

Writing Tip

You should also use **leads in longer pieces of writing**, such as stories, reports, and articles. In longer pieces of writing, a lead may be an entire paragraph. The type of lead you use depends on the type of writing.

- For four dark hours, I had crouched shivering and waiting in the duck blind. (story)
- Biologists know that birds have wings, but few have asked why. (article)

PROOFREADING

Proofreading is the process of finding and correcting errors in written work. Use **proofreading symbols** to note the changes that you want to make in your writing.

Proofreading Symbols	Meanings	Examples
≡	Change a small letter to a capital.	capitalize the first letter.
/	Change a capital letter to a small one.	Make a Small Letter.
¶	Begin a new paragraph.	¶ Start a new paragraph when the main idea changes.
ℒ	Delete this letter, word, punctuation mark, or sentence.	Take out any extra or incorrect letters, words words, punctuation marks, or sentences.
∧	Add a missing letter or word.	Put in one or more words or letters.
∿ tr	Transpose the letters or words.	Letters or words be should in the correct order.
… STET	Let it stand.	Don't delete this word. STET
∧ (comma)	Insert a comma.	Ann put a comma here please.
⊙	Insert a period.	This is the end⊙
∧ (semicolon)	Insert a semicolon.	Join these clauses insert a semicolon.
?	Insert a question mark.	Where does the question mark go?
∨	Add an apostrophe.	Abes name needs an apostrophe.
" "	Add quotation marks.	Please don't forget the quotation marks, said Mrs. Speaks.

Here is how one writer marked changes in a paragraph.

The panda is found in china and Tibet. It lives in bamboo forests on mountain slopes. The ~~very~~ giant panda resembles a bear in shape size. It has white body and black legs. Black patchs ring the Pandas eyes. Bamboo shoots is this animals favorite food. like bears, pandas walk slow. ~~Chinese laws protect some animals.~~ The red panda is different quite from giant panda. The red panda looks more like a fox its fur is soft and orange. Its full, bushy tail has rings like a raccoons. When I first saw a panda, I said, wow

The following paragraphs need 30 changes, including the deletion of an unrelated detail. Use proofreader's symbols to note the corrections that should be made.

Antarctica is an extremely frigid and forbidding region. This Continent surrounds the South Pole and is mostly covered with with snow, and ice.

Antarcticas coast support many forms of life Fish, whales, penguins, and seals all here live. these animals depend on the ocean for there food. Rocky hills support only the roughest forms of life. Few humans visited antarctica until the 1800s. Then a few of the most bravest explorers begin to travel across the continent. A number of they perished in theirs attempts to reach the South pole. Today, Scientists have research Bases, in Antarctica. They hope to answer many questions. they ask, "When did Antarctica become ice covered They had also asked, "Does the land contain any valuable natural resources

Rewrite correctly the paragraphs about Antarctica.

PREPARE FOR A TEST

Read this article about an archaeological discovery.
Then answer questions 1–18.

King Tut's Tomb

(1) Tutankhamen was born around 1343 B.C. (2) By the age of 9, he had become pharaoh of ancient egypt. (3) By the age of 19, he had died. (4) Whom could have guessed that the young king's greatest fame would begin more than 3,000 years later?

(5) The ancient Egyptians believed in an afterlife. (6) They thought that the dead traveled to the next world using the body they have in life. (7) Therefore, the preservative of the body was of special importance. (8) The body was embalmed and tightly wrapped in strips of cloth. (9) Many pharaohs and there families were buried in massive pyramids at Giza, on the banks of the Nile River.

(10) In the early 1900s, archaeologist Howard Carter began an excavation, he was searching for Tutankhamen's tomb. (11) For over 15 years, Carter's excavations met with frustration. (12) He discovered four royal tombs in the Valley of the king's, but tomb robbers had looted all of the tombs.

(13) On November 4, 1922 Carter's crew uncovered the top step of a buried stairway. (14) After clearing the 16 steps, he faced a blocked doorway that bore the seals of Tutankhamen. (15) One seal depicted a wolf profile. (16) Carter and his team continued with most painstakingest care to dig their way in. (17) Three months later, they reached the burial chamber.

(18) This chamber contained a golden throne, chests filled with clothing and jewelry, an ebony chair, and three shrines covered with ancient Egyptian writing which is called "hieroglyphics." (19) The largest shrine was so immense that it took 84 days to dismantle. (20) Nested one inside the other, this shrine held three coffins. (21) The innermost coffin, the farthest inside, was pure gold. (22) Within that gold coffin lay the mummy of Tutankhamen hisself, wearing a golden mask. (23) King Tut had been found at last! (24) Howard Carter went on to write and publish *the Tomb of Tut-ank-amen*, a three-volume record of the stunning discovery that was the highlight of his career.

1. What change should be made in sentence 2?
   - Ⓐ Change *he* to *He*.
   - Ⓑ Change *egypt* to *Egypt*.
   - Ⓒ Change *ancient* to *Ancient*.
   - Ⓓ Change *age* to *Age*.

2. What change would correct sentence 4?
   - Ⓐ Change *Whom* to *Who*.
   - Ⓑ Change *Whom* to *Which*.
   - Ⓒ Change *Whom* to *You*.
   - Ⓓ Change *Whom* to *He*.

3. Which verb should replace *have* in sentence 6?
   - Ⓐ *had*.
   - Ⓑ *might have had*.
   - Ⓒ *would have had*.
   - Ⓓ *have had*.

4. Which suffix change should be made in sentence 7?
   - Ⓐ Change *preservative* to *preserves*.
   - Ⓑ Change *preservative* to *preservation*.
   - Ⓒ Change *special* to *specialness*.
   - Ⓓ Change *special* to *specialty*.

5. What change should be made in sentence 9?
   - Ⓐ Change *there* to *they're*.
   - Ⓑ Change *there* to *theyre*.
   - Ⓒ Change *there* to *there's*.
   - Ⓓ Change *there* to *their*.

6. What is the best way to rewrite sentence 10?
   - Ⓐ In the early 1900s, archaeologist Howard Carter was searching for Tutankhamen's tomb, he began an excavation.
   - Ⓑ In the early 1900s, archaeologist Howard Carter began an excavation. He was searching for Tutankhamen's tomb.
   - Ⓒ Archaeologist Howard Carter began an excavation, he was searching for Tutankhamen's tomb in the early 1900s.
   - Ⓓ Searching, for Tutankhamen's tomb in the early 1900s, archaeologist Howard Carter began an excavation.

7. In sentence 12, *Valley of the king's* should be changed to
   Ⓐ *Valley of the kings'.*
   Ⓑ *Valley of the Kings.*
   Ⓒ *valley of the kings.*
   Ⓓ *Valley Of The Kings.*

8. Sentence 12 would be improved by
   Ⓐ deleting *of the tombs.*
   Ⓑ changing the second use of the word *tombs* to *them.*
   Ⓒ changing *all of the tombs* to *all the tombs.*
   Ⓓ inserting a comma after *all.*

9. What change should be made in sentence 13?
   Ⓐ Delete the comma after *4.*
   Ⓑ Insert a comma after *1922.*
   Ⓒ Rewrite the date as *11/4/22.*
   Ⓓ Rewrite the date as *4 November 1922.*

10. To make sentence 14 clearer, *he* should be changed to
    Ⓐ *they.*
    Ⓑ *them.*
    Ⓒ *it.*
    Ⓓ *we.*

11. In sentence 15, it would be correct to change *wolf* to
    Ⓐ *wolfs'.*
    Ⓑ *wolf's.*
    Ⓒ *wolfs.*
    Ⓓ *wolfses.*

12. What change should be made in sentence 16?
    Ⓐ Change *painstakingest* to *painstakinger.*
    Ⓑ Change *painstakingest* to *painstakingness.*
    Ⓒ Change *most painstakingest* to *painstaking.*
    Ⓓ Change *most painstakingest* to *most painstakingly.*

13. What change would improve sentence 18?
    - Ⓐ Delete the comma after *throne*.
    - Ⓑ Delete the comma after *jewelry*.
    - Ⓒ Insert a comma after *writing*.
    - Ⓓ Insert a comma after *ancient*.

14. What change, if any, should be made in sentence 20 to place modifiers correctly?
    - Ⓐ This shrine held nested one inside the other, three coffins.
    - Ⓑ This shrine held nested, one inside, the other three coffins.
    - Ⓒ This shrine held three coffins nested one inside the other.
    - Ⓓ Make no change.

15. In sentence 21, what is unnecessary and should be eliminated?
    - Ⓐ *was pure gold*
    - Ⓑ *the farthest inside*
    - Ⓒ *coffin*
    - Ⓓ *gold*

16. What change should be made to sentence 22?
    - Ⓐ Change *golden* to *golder*.
    - Ⓑ Change *hisself* to *herself*.
    - Ⓒ Change *hisself* to *himself*.
    - Ⓓ Change *hisself* to *theirself*.

17. What correction should be made to the title in sentence 24?
    - Ⓐ As the first word of the title, *The* should be capitalized.
    - Ⓑ The word *of* should be capitalized.
    - Ⓒ The words *the* and *of* should be capitalized.
    - Ⓓ The word *Tomb* should *not* be capitalized.

18. In the last paragraph, which detail sentence is *least* relevant to the main idea?
    - Ⓐ Sentence 20.
    - Ⓑ Sentence 22.
    - Ⓒ Sentence 23.
    - Ⓓ Sentence 24.

*Read this essay about self-defense in the insect world.
Then answer questions 19–36.*

Buzz Off

(1) Insects are among the most intriguing creatures on earth. (2) Their fascinating characteristics include remarkable methods of protective self-defense. (3) Like all creatures that must defend themselves. (4) Insects have a weird understanding that alertness is a means of self-protection. (5) Maybe that is why some insects has so many eyes. (6) Arachnids, including spiders, have as many as eight.

(7) Insects whom are weaker than their enemies often use the tactic of disguise. (8) Imitating the appearance of their surroundings, they defend themselves with camouflage. (9) When such insects are stationery, they're rarely seen by enemies. (10) The kallima, a tropical leaf butterfly, looks like a brown leaf. (11) Into the tree bark on which it sits the peppered moth blends. (12) The northern walkingstick resembles a green stem or a twig. (13) The waterscorpion is easily mistaken for a floating stick. (14) The thorn-mimic treehopper imitates a thorn. (15) Any enemy of bugs like these are likely to pass by without noticing.

(16) Other insects, such as the Io moth and the pearly eye butterfly, defend theyselves with another type of deception. (17) They have a characteristic known as eyespots. (18) An eyespot are a large marking that looks like an eye. (19) The appearance of enormous, multiple eyes frightened away some would-be predators, such as birds. (20) Color is another device that some insects use to fend off unfriendly creatures. (21) The colors red and yellow send a warning true or false, that the colored insect either stings or tastes bad. (22) On traffic lights and signs, red and yellow are also warning colors. (23) Because of the red hourglass shape on its abdomen. (24) The female black widow spider is left alone by nearly every creature except it's unfortunate mate!

(25) What can one conclude about appearances in the insect world? (26) Looks may be deceiving. (27) But in a bug's life, they can be a matter of life and death.

19. What change, if any, should be made in sentence 1?
    - Ⓐ Insert a comma after *most*.
    - Ⓑ Underline the sentence.
    - Ⓒ Replace the period with a question mark.
    - Ⓓ Make no change.

20. In sentence 2, which word is unnecessary and should be deleted?
    - Ⓐ *characteristics*
    - Ⓑ *remarkable*
    - Ⓒ *protective*
    - Ⓓ *self-defense*

21. What change should be made to sentence 3?
    - Ⓐ Add a comma after *themselves* and join the fragment to the beginning of sentence 4.
    - Ⓑ Add a period after *creatures* and break the fragment into two sentences.
    - Ⓒ Change *themselves* to *theirselves*.
    - Ⓓ Change *that* to *who*.

22. In sentence 5, the verb *has* should be changed to
    - Ⓐ *have had*.
    - Ⓑ *are having*.
    - Ⓒ *had*.
    - Ⓓ *have*.

23. What change should be made in sentence 7?
    - Ⓐ Change *whom* to *who*.
    - Ⓑ Change *whom* to *that*.
    - Ⓒ Insert a comma before *whom*.
    - Ⓓ Insert a comma after *enemies*.

24. In sentence 9, what change should be made?
    - Ⓐ Change *stationery* to *stationary*.
    - Ⓑ Change *they're* to *there*.
    - Ⓒ Change *seen* to *scene*.
    - Ⓓ Change *by* to *buy*.

25. How would sentence 11 look if it were written correctly?
    Ⓐ The peppered moth blends into the tree bark on which it sits.
    Ⓑ The peppered moth on which sits the tree bark blends into it.
    Ⓒ The tree bark blends into the peppered moth on which it sits.
    Ⓓ The tree bark sits on the peppered moth that blends into it.

26. What change, if any, should be made in sentence 12?
    Ⓐ Insert a comma after *green.*
    Ⓑ Capitalize *green.*
    Ⓒ Change *northern* to *north.*
    Ⓓ Make no change.

27. What change should be made in sentence 15?
    Ⓐ Change *pass* to *be passing.*
    Ⓑ Change *are* to *is.*
    Ⓒ Change *pass* to *fly.*
    Ⓓ Change *bugs* to *a bug.*

28. In sentence 16, *theyselves* should be changed to
    Ⓐ *itself.*
    Ⓑ *theirselves.*
    Ⓒ *themselves.*
    Ⓓ *itselfs.*

29. What change should be made in sentence 18?
    Ⓐ Change *look* to *looks.*
    Ⓑ Change *eye* to *eyes.*
    Ⓒ Change *are* to *is.*
    Ⓓ Insert a comma after *marking.*

30. In sentence 19, the verb *frightened* should be changed to
    Ⓐ *frightening.*
    Ⓑ *frighten.*
    Ⓒ *had frightened.*
    Ⓓ *frightens.*

31. Sentence 20 should be
    (A) deleted.
    (B) indented, starting a new paragraph.
    (C) divided, making two separate sentences.
    (D) underlined.

32. In sentence 21, a comma should be inserted
    (A) after *colors*.
    (B) after *yellow*.
    (C) after *warning*.
    (D) after *true*.

33. Sentence 22 does not belong in the paragraph because
    (A) it does not support the main idea of the paragraph.
    (B) it contains incorrect information.
    (C) it is a fragment.
    (D) it is incorrectly punctuated.

34. To create a complex sentence, how should sentences 23 and 24 be changed?
    (A) No changes should be made to either sentence.
    (B) Sentence 23 should be followed by a comma and joined to the beginning of sentence 24.
    (C) Sentence 23 should be joined to the beginning of sentence 24, with no additional punctuation.
    (D) Sentence 23 should be deleted.

35. What change should be made in sentence 24?
    (A) Insert a comma after *alone*.
    (B) Delete the apostrophe in *it's*.
    (C) Place the apostrophe after the *s* in *it's*.
    (D) Delete the exclamation mark.

36. What change would make sentence 27 more effective?
    (A) Insert a comma after *matter*.
    (B) Delete the comma after *life*.
    (C) Split it into two sentences, replacing the comma after *life* with a period.
    (D) Precede it with a comma and join it to sentence 26, making a compound sentence.

Read this short history of the bicycle. Then answer questions 37–54.

The Bike

(1) Like most machines, the bicycle did not enter the world in its present form. (2) The first bicycle was invented in France nearly 200 years ago. (3) It was made of wood. (4) It had no steering wheel or pedals. (5) It looked like a scooter.

(6) In 1872, an all-metal bicycle with wheels, is designed in England. (7) It had a real huge front wheel and a small back wheel. (8) Not surprisingly inventists soon added features such as same-sized wheels, rubber tires, and gears. (9) By the turn of the twentieth century, the bicycle resembled the vehicle that you and me ourselfs know today.

(10) The word *bicycle*, that is from a French word meaning "two-wheeled," is only one of many names that have been given to this machine. (11) In English, the first bike was called a dandy horse or walk-along. (12) The high-wheeled model, which was more higher, was called the "high-wheeler."

(13) The popularity of the bicycle has sure risen and fallen over the years. (14) In the early 1900s, the bicycle became the first luxury product to be widely advertised. (15) In those days, bicycles were extremely popular, many indoor cycling arenas were built. (16) Teams of cyclists competed in events and were earning good salaries. (17) With the rise of the automobile, however, many people became less interested in riding bicycles, especially in the United States. (18) However, during World war II, gas shortages led to another increase in bicycle use.

(19) Today, a concern with health and exercise has given a fresh boost to the bicycle market. (20) In addition, the popularity of cycling as a spectator's sport has enjoyed a revival. (21) Cycling has become a favorite event in the Olympics. (22) An international cycling competition is held every Summer in France and it attracts avid spectators. (23) The Tour de France. (24) Fans around the world watches its racing events on television. (25) It appears from such widespread enthusiasm that the sporty, economical, and environmentally sound bicycle is here to stay.

37. Which statement best describes sentence 1?
    Ⓐ   It contains faulty punctuation.
    Ⓑ   It is a fragment.
    Ⓒ   It is a run-on sentence.
    Ⓓ   It is a good lead.

38. To provide variety, which is the best combination of sentences 4 and 5?
    Ⓐ   It looked like a scooter, it had no steering wheel or pedals.
    Ⓑ   Having no steering wheel or pedals. It looked like a scooter.
    Ⓒ   Since it had no steering wheel or pedals, it looked like a scooter.
    Ⓓ   It had no steering wheel or pedals, it looked like a scooter.

39. What change should be made in sentence 6?
    Ⓐ   Delete the comma after *1872*.
    Ⓑ   Place a comma before *England*.
    Ⓒ   End the sentence with a question mark.
    Ⓓ   Delete the comma after *wheels*.

40. The verb in sentence 6 should be changed to
    Ⓐ   *has been designed.*
    Ⓑ   *will be designed.*
    Ⓒ   *was designed.*
    Ⓓ   *could have been designed.*

41. Which change should be made to sentence 7?
    Ⓐ   Change *real* to *really*.
    Ⓑ   Add *most* before *real*.
    Ⓒ   Change *real* to *realer*.
    Ⓓ   Change *real* to *realest*.

42. Which change, if any, should be made in sentence 8?
    Ⓐ   Change *inventists* to *invents*.
    Ⓑ   Change *inventists* to *inventors*.
    Ⓒ   Change *inventists* to *invention*.
    Ⓓ   Make no change.

43. What punctuation change should be made in sentence 8?
   Ⓐ Delete the comma after *wheels*.
   Ⓑ Replace the period with a question mark.
   Ⓒ Add a comma after *surprisingly*.
   Ⓓ Add a comma after *as*.

44. The best revision of sentence 9 is
   Ⓐ By the turn of the twentieth century, the bicycle resembled the vehicle that we ourselfs know today.
   Ⓑ By the turn of the twentieth century, the bicycle resembled the vehicle that we know today.
   Ⓒ By the turn of the twentieth century the bicycle resembled the vehicle that we know today, you and me.
   Ⓓ You and I ourselves today are reminded of the bicycle of the twentieth century.

45. In sentence 10, the word *that*
   Ⓐ should be replaced with *which*.
   Ⓑ is correct.
   Ⓒ should be deleted.
   Ⓓ should not follow a comma.

46. Which punctuation change should be made in sentence 11?
   Ⓐ Delete the comma after *English*.
   Ⓑ Enclose *bike* in quotation marks.
   Ⓒ Enclose *dandy horse* in quotation marks.
   Ⓓ Enclose *dandy horse* and *walk-along* in quotation marks.

47. What change should be made in sentence 12?
   Ⓐ Delete the comma before *which*.
   Ⓑ Place the final quotation mark before the period.
   Ⓒ Delete the word *more*.
   Ⓓ Change *higher* to *highest*.

48. What change should be made in sentence 13?
   Ⓐ Do not indent the sentence.
   Ⓑ Change *risen* to *rised*.
   Ⓒ Change *years* to *year*.
   Ⓓ Change *sure* to *surely*.

49. Which is a correct revision of run-on sentence 15?
    Ⓐ In those days. Bicycles were extremely popular. Many indoor cycling arenas. Were built.
    Ⓑ In those days, bicycles were extremely popular. Many indoor cycling arenas were built.
    Ⓒ In those days bicycles were extremely popular many indoor cycling arenas were built.
    Ⓓ In those days, bicycles were extremely popular, many indoor, cycling arenas were built.

50. What change should be made in sentence 16 to create parallel structure?
    Ⓐ Change *competed* to *competing*.
    Ⓑ Change *were earning* to *was earning*.
    Ⓒ Change *were earning* to *are earning*.
    Ⓓ Change *were earning* to *earned*.

51. What change or changes should be made in sentence 18?
    Ⓐ Change *World war II* to *World War II*.
    Ⓑ Change *World war II* to *World War 2*.
    Ⓒ Change *World war II* to *world War II*.
    Ⓓ Change *World war II* to *world war II*.

52. In sentence 22, which capitalization change should be made?
    Ⓐ Do not capitalize *Summer*.
    Ⓑ Do not capitalize *France*.
    Ⓒ Do not capitalize *An*.
    Ⓓ Capitalize *cycling*.

53. Which is the best combination of sentences 22 and 23?
    Ⓐ An international cycling competition the Tour de France, is held every summer in France and it attracts avid spectators.
    Ⓑ An international cycling competition, the Tour de France, is held every summer in France, and it attracts avid spectators.
    Ⓒ An international cycling competition, is held every summer in France, the Tour de France, and it attracts avid spectators.
    Ⓓ An international cycling competition, is held every summer in France, the Tour de France and it attracts avid spectators.

54. What change should be made in sentence 24?
    Ⓐ Change *world* to *World*.
    Ⓑ Change *its* to *it's*.
    Ⓒ Change *watches* to *watch*.
    Ⓓ Change *television* to *Television*.

DESCRIPTIVE ESSAYS

A description creates mental impressions of people, places, or things. In a descriptive essay, you use carefully chosen details and descriptive language to create vivid images in readers' minds.

Here is a sample prompt for a descriptive essay.

> *Write an essay describing a place where you feel good.*

Read this descriptive essay, which was written in response to the prompt. Then read the Writing Tips to learn more about descriptive essays.

Writing Tips

* Show instead of tell. When you describe a person, place, or thing, remember that readers need your specific words and details to help them experience what they don't know. Make them feel as though they are experiencing your subject with you as they read.

* Before writing, think about your five senses to generate sensory details that will make images of the subject come vividly to life in your readers' minds. When describing a place, ask yourself: What can I see and hear there? Can I smell, taste, or touch anything? Jot down whatever comes to mind.

* Carefully choose the most precise adjectives, adverbs, nouns, and verbs to build the description.

* Order your details in a way that makes sense: by time, position, or importance, for example.

* Occasionally use figurative language, such as similes or metaphors, to develop aspects of your images. If there are dry leaves on the ground, do they "rustle like rushing water"?

* Give your description a catchy title and a clear beginning, middle, and ending.

The Cabin

Every August, we visit a log cabin in northern California. It's small and low and has a wide front porch, dark green shutters, and a stone chimney. It crouches there in the woods, looking like an old friend who has been waiting for us to arrive.

As we turn off the two-lane road, my heart always pounds when the cabin comes into view. I can hardly wait to jump from the car and breathe that fresh air that smells and tastes like pine. The ground will be springy with a layer of pine needles that crunch lightly under my feet. The blue jays and chipmunks will make a racket. It's like they are scolding us for the invasion.

As soon as Dad gets the front door open, my brother and I burst through. We blast past the sitting room, still dark from the winter shutters. The wooden staircase is worn and steep, but we race up. On the landing, we wedge side-by-side in the doorway of our familiar knotty-pine room. It looks and smells like home. To the left and right of the window, two narrow beds are neatly made and plumped as high as hills. We gaze at them in anticipation. We have come for those mattresses, stuffed with goose down!

My brother and I exchange silent looks and step to our positions at the foot of our beds. We holler, "One! Two! Three!" and dive through the air. The next second we're sinking, feather by feather, into the most comfortable place on earth.

USING GRAPHIC ORGANIZERS

Before you write, use graphic organizers to help yourself gather and sort information for your description.

The writer of the descriptive essay about the cabin on page 76 might have used a Sensory Words Chart, such as the one below.

Sight	wide front porch, dark green shutters, stone chimney, two-lane road, dark sitting room, wooden staircase, knotty-pine room, narrow beds high as hills, mattresses
Sound	pine needles crunching lightly; blue jays and chipmunks making a racket; scolding; hollering
Taste	fresh air that smells and tastes like pine
Touch	crunch lightly; springy ground; my heart pounds; wedge side-by-side; sink, feather by feather
Smell	air smells like pine; room smells like home

A Sensory Words Chart helps writers gather and organize details related to some or all of the five senses. The details can then be used to create vivid images in descriptive writing.

The writer of the description on page 76 might also have used a Descriptive Details Cluster such as the one below. If you had been the writer, what descriptive details would you have used to create strong images of the cabin in the woods? Fill in the ovals with descriptive details.

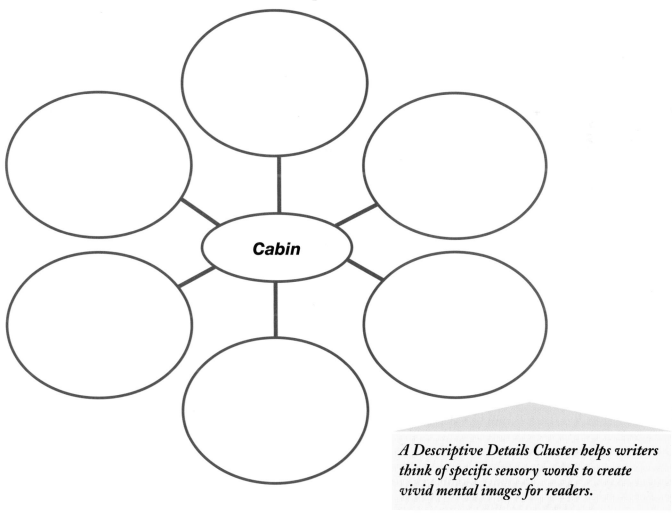

A Descriptive Details Cluster helps writers think of specific sensory words to create vivid mental images for readers.

Score: 4

Read the descriptive essay below, which was written in response to the prompt on page 76. This description scored a 4 on a scale from 1 to 4 (with 4 being the best). Then read the comments and think about why this description scored a 4.

Aqua Maureen

My name is Maureen, and my favorite sport is snorkeling. I'm lucky because every summer I get to snorkel above a tropical reef. I love the way it makes me feel. When I wade into the lapping surf, it is as warm as a blanket. I adjust my mask and snorkel. Then I bend at the knees and go under until my ears are submerged. Under the water, all I can hear is my breath, drawing in and blowing out.

I start to relax, face down in the shallow water, letting myself float. My hands touch the coarse sand and reach for coral outcroppings to pull me along. The rubber fins on my feet paddle so easily that I hardly have to try. I drift along, as weightless as a sea creature, following the current and my curiosity.

The mask feels tight, but it keeps the water out so I can see the fish, which are everywhere. They hover and then flash away. My favorite fish are bright yellow with a black spot under each eye. The anemones are interesting, too, with tiny pink tentacles that wiggle like fingers. Once I saw a spotted eel which looked like a snake with teeth. It darted its head out from a little cave, but I kept my distance!

Marine time passes so gradually that you hardly notice. When its time to come in, I always feel ridiculously heavy, tall, and clumsy as I first stand up. Because the fins make it hard to wade in any direction but backwards, I stagger and splash. In the cool air, my skin develops goose bumps. The call of sea gulls sounds too loud. Unfortunately, I'm back on land again.

Your Turn

Now it's your turn to help the writer. Find and fix the errors in the writing. Go back to the pages in green if you need help.

1. Find and fix the nonessential clause that should be set off by a **comma**. The clause begins with *which*. See pp. 12–13, 30–31, 36–37, and 52–53.

2. Find and fix the **contraction** error. See pp. 54–55.

TEACHER COMMENTS 4

▲ Your title is catchy. Good!

▲ I can easily imagine the reef and the snorkeling experience from your sensory words and details.

▲ Your simile comparing the eel to "a snake with teeth" is perfect! No wonder you kept your distance!

▲ You've done a nice job of varying your sentence structure.

▲ The order of organization (entering, exploring, leaving marine setting) works really well.

▲ You have written an effective closing.

PARTNER COMMENTS 3

Your description came totally alive in my mind. I felt like I was at the reef myself. Great description.

Read the descriptive essay and the comments that follow. Think about why this description scored a 3.

1

Above the Reef

Snorkeling is my favorite thing to do. The water over the reef is always real warm. I go in, and most of the sounds around me disappear. When I put my ears underwater, I only hear my breath.

I float in the shallow water, and my hands grab things to pull me along. My feet wear fins like a duck. I paddle along with the current, but I will be swimming in other directions when I see something interesting.

My mask feels funny but it helps me see the fish and the fish are everywhere, and I never really know how they will move. They never seem stationery. I might see anemones waving like tiny fingers. I might see an eel, but it could be dangerous. If I see an eel peeking from a hole, I get out of the way fast!

When it's time to go in, somehow I always know. When I stand up out of the water, I feel kind of funny. The fins, my heaviest piece of equipment make me stumble. I'm cold. I'm back on land again.

2

PARTNER COMMENTS

Your description got my attention, but you could have used more details and some words that told more about what it's like to be underwater. Your sentences were a little choppy. Your ideas were in an order that made sense, though.

3

Your Turn

Now it's your turn to help the writer. Find and fix the errors in the writing. Go back to the pages in green if you need help.

1. Find and fix the **adjective** that should be an **adverb**. See pp. 26–27.
2. Find and fix the error in **inconsistent verb tense**. See pp. 42–43.
3. Find and fix the **rambling sentence**. See pp. 40–41.
4. Find and fix the incorrect **homophone**. See pp. 28–29.
5. Find and fix the **appositive** that is missing a **comma**. See pp. 38–39.

TEACHER COMMENTS

4

▲ Because you introduced the subject in your title and opening paragraph, I know what you are going to describe.

▲ Your details are arranged in a logical sequence, into and then out of the water.

▲ It's nice that you're including some comparisons, but make sure they make sense. Does a duck wear fins? Is it anemones, or their tentacles, that wave?

▲ You use a variety of kinds of sentences, but your sentences could flow more smoothly. Try including some **transitional words**, such as *then* and *next*. See pp. 60–61 for help.

▲ You make some nice word choices, but you could use more **sensory words** to enliven your description. In what way does your mask feel "funny"? Does it scratch your face? Is there water in it? See pp. 58–59.

Score:

2

Read the descriptive essay and the comments that follow. Think about why this description scored a 2.

1

I can only hear my breath under the water. Most sounds disappears. I float in the water. I grab things to move along. I wear fins. And a mask.

I feel great snorkeling. There are many fish and anemones and an eel and eels can be dangerous, so you should get out of there way fast. The Reef invite you to come on in. When it's time to go out, you'll no. I try standing up, but it isnt easy. I way too much. Then I fall down. It is the fins. I hear the gulls's sounds. Im in the air again. Because it is very cold. I want to be in the water again.

2

PARTNER COMMENTS

I could tell that you were talking about snorkeling, but you didn't really describe a place. Many sentences were too short and rushed. Better details would have helped.

3

Your Turn

Now it's your turn to help the writer. Find and fix the errors in the writing. Go back to the pages in green if you need help.

1. Find and fix the two errors in **subject-verb agreement**. See pp. 18–19.

2. Find and fix the two **sentence fragments**. See pp. 34–35.

3. Find and fix the **rambling sentence**. See pp. 40–41.

4. Find and fix the three incorrect **homophones**. See pp. 28–29.

5. Find and fix the **capitalization** error. See pp. 48–49.

6. Find and fix the two **contraction** errors. See pp. 54–55.

7. Find and fix the incorrect **possessive noun**. See pp. 8–9.

TEACHER COMMENTS

4

▲ Please add a title to your descriptive essay.

▲ You do include some details, but to form strong images, the reader needs to know more. Take your time and add enough details to create a vivid description.

▲ Your description includes both *I* and *you*. Use one or the other.

▲ The parts of your description don't follow a logical order. This makes it hard for me to read. You want to hold, not lose, your readers' attention.

▲ Can you give more variety to the **structure** of your **sentences**? Many sentences begin with *I*. Try **joining** some of the short **sentences**. See pp. 36–37 for help.

▲ Use more **descriptive words** so that readers will form images in their minds. See pp. 22–23.

▲ Try to use more **sensory words** to enliven your descriptions. See pp. 58–59.

Score:

Read the descriptive essay and the comments that follow. Think about why this description scored a 1.

My sister always talks about the beach. She go there. With her friend Liz. I dont know why. I like the mall. My sister and me disagrees sometimes she says she likes the beach, but I think she just like lying around in the sun she never swims or snorkels. I would like to snorkel. At a reef. One time my sister and myself went to Walton beach. That was the most hottest day of the year. She got in the water then. I was really like totally surprised. Thats all I can tell you.

PARTNER COMMENTS

Your essay needs a title. I wasn't sure what your subject was. It was hard to picture anything because your ideas jumped all around. You needed better organization.

TEACHER COMMENTS

▲ The essay should describe a place that makes you feel good. Please follow the prompt.

▲ Your description needs a more specific beginning, middle, and ending. Your thoughts wander; you should order them better.

▲ Your **main idea and details** should be connected and should lead logically from one to another. Use more **transitional words** or **phrases**. See pp. 58–59 and 60–61 for help.

▲ Use some **sensory words** that give more specifics about the beach so that readers can get a picture of it in their minds. See pp 58–59.

▲ Try using more **variety** in your **sentences**. See pp. 30–31, 36–37, and 44–45.

▲ Create a paragraph for each new idea, and indent each **paragraph**. See pp. 58–59.

Your Turn

Now it's your turn to help the writer. Find and fix the errors in the writing. Go back to the pages in green if you need help.

1. Find and fix the two errors in **subject-verb agreement**. See pp. 18–19.

2. Find and fix the two **sentence fragments**. See pp. 34–35.

3. Find and fix the two **contraction** errors. See pp. 54–55.

4. Find and fix the **rambling sentence**. See pp. 40–41.

5. Find and fix the incorrect **subject pronoun**. See pp. 10–11.

6. Find and fix the incorrect **reflexive pronoun**. See pp. 14–15.

7. Find and fix the **capitalization** error. See pp. 48–49.

8. Find and fix the **double comparison**. See pp. 22–23.

9. Find and fix the **unnecessary phrase**. See pp. 42–43.

USING A RUBRIC TO SCORE DESCRIPTIVE ESSAYS

This rubric is based on a point scale of 1 to 4. It was used to score the descriptive essays on pages 78–81. Use the rubric to remember what is important in descriptive essays.

4 A score of *4* means that the writer

- ❑ connects the writing directly to the prompt.
- ❑ almost always uses the correct forms of words.
- ❑ almost always uses capitalization and punctuation correctly.
- ❑ almost always uses clear and complete sentences and uses variety in sentences.
- ❑ creates a title that clearly relates to the description.
- ❑ introduces the subject clearly at the beginning.
- ❑ creates a description with a clear beginning, middle, and ending.
- ❑ uses interesting details and sensory words to create strong images for readers.
- ❑ uses comparisons, if they strengthen the imagery.
- ❑ uses an appropriate system of organization, such as spatial order.
- ❑ begins a new paragraph for each change of idea or speaker.

2 A score of *2* means that the writer

- ❑ connects the writing to the prompt in a general way.
- ❑ uses some incorrect forms of words.
- ❑ makes some errors in capitalization or punctuation.
- ❑ uses little sentence variety and uses some run-on or rambling sentences or sentence fragments.
- ❑ usually creates a title that relates in some way to the description.
- ❑ presents the subject somewhere within the description.
- ❑ creates a description with a weak beginning, middle, or ending.
- ❑ uses too few interesting details or sensory words to create strong images for readers.
- ❑ uses no comparisons or uses them unsuccessfully.
- ❑ uses a weak system of organization.
- ❑ may make some paragraphing errors.

3 A score of *3* means that the writer

- ❑ connects the writing to the prompt.
- ❑ usually uses the correct forms of words.
- ❑ usually uses capitalization and punctuation correctly.
- ❑ usually uses clear and complete sentences and uses some sentence variety.
- ❑ creates a title that relates to the description.
- ❑ introduces the subject toward the beginning.
- ❑ creates a description with a beginning, middle, and ending.
- ❑ uses some interesting details and sensory words to create images for readers.
- ❑ uses some simple comparisons to strengthen the imagery.
- ❑ uses an adequate system of organization.
- ❑ usually begins a new paragraph for each change of idea or speaker.

1 A score of *1* means that the writer

- ❑ does not successfully connect the writing to the prompt.
- ❑ uses many incorrect forms of words.
- ❑ makes several errors in capitalization or punctuation.
- ❑ uses almost no sentence variety and uses several run-on or rambling sentences or sentence fragments.
- ❑ usually creates a poor title or has no title at all.
- ❑ identifies the subject in an unclear way or not at all.
- ❑ creates a description without a clear beginning, middle, or ending.
- ❑ uses words and details that fail to create strong images for readers.
- ❑ uses no comparisons.
- ❑ uses an inadequate system of organization.
- ❑ may make many paragraphing errors.

SCORING DESCRIPTIVE ESSAYS

Now it's your turn to score some descriptive essays. The four descriptive essays on pages 83 and 84 were written in response to this prompt.

> *Write an essay describing a specific person's face.*

Read each descriptive essay. Write a few comments about it and then give it a score from 1 to 4. Think about what you've learned in this lesson as you match each description with its correct score.

Model A

Score:

A Writer's Face

I was at the Smithtown Public library. I saw a picture of someone with a face like I don't see every day. It was a writer named Samuel Beckett. His face made me stop to look at it real close.

Mr. Beckett's hair was gray, short on the sides, and longer on top. You could hardly tell that his eyes were blue because they were so light. His forehead had deep wrinkles, and his eyebrows were bushy and his nose was like a beak.

Beckett reminded me of some kind of angry bird. His face made me sort of think of that. But maybe he couldnt help it.

Comments: _____

_____

_____

_____

_____

_____

_____

Model B

Score:

The library is where I go after school, its in Smithtown on Taylor Street. I always sits at the same table I seen a book their with a picture of a writer Mr Bekett. That man looks mad maybe he had a bad time. I finished my homework and then went home. When I got home we will have supper and Im ready myselfs.

Comments: _____

_____

_____

_____

_____

_____

_____

Model C

Score:

A Look on a Book

After school, at the Smithtown Public Library, I noticed a book on the table. It showed a picture of the author Samuel Beckett. His face practically jumped out at me, so I stopped, and looked closer.

Beckett had silver hair, which was cut short above his ears. On top it was longer and scrunched up, like a crown of feathers. His forehead had rows of wrinkles across it. His eyebrows stuck out like another set of plumes. His pale blue eyes seemed to be sharply focused on something. His nose was like an enormous beak, and it cast a shadow across his mouth. He was frowning as if he had invented the frown!

I wondered how someone could develop a face like that. What had Mr. Beckett been thinking all his life? He looked like a wild eagle.

Comments: _____

_____

_____

_____

_____

_____

_____

_____

Model D

Score:

I was at the library. I seen a book with a picture of Mr. Samuel Beckett who was a writer. He wrote books and plays. But I havent seen any of them. I was just sitting at the table when I saw it. Then I got to looking at the picture. Mr. beckett did not look not even one little bit happy in that picture, he looked kind of mad or sad or something you couldnt tell for sure. He had gray hair. He looked like some kind of animal, like the way some people look like there a dog or a cat. Only he didnt look like one of them.

Comments: _____

_____

_____

_____

_____

_____

_____

_____

WRITING A DESCRIPTIVE ESSAY

Now you get to write your own descriptive essay. Use the prompt below.

> *Write an essay describing a place where you like to spend time.*

When You Write Your Descriptive Essay

1. **Think about** what you want to write. Close your eyes and think about the place you want to describe. Ask yourself some questions.
   - What do I see and hear there?
   - What can I touch and what does it feel like?
   - Can I smell or taste anything there?

   Use graphic organizers to gather and sort the information.

2. **Write** your first draft. Your descriptive essay should be four to five paragraphs long and should have a clear and effective beginning, middle, and ending.

3. **Read** your draft. Use the checklist that your teacher will give you to review your writing.

4. **Edit** your essay. Make changes until your description creates strong images.

5. **Proofread** your descriptive essay one last time.

6. **Write** a neat copy of your descriptive essay and give it to your partner.

Work with a Partner

7. **Read** your partner's descriptive essay.

8. **Score** your partner's descriptive essay from 1 to 4, using the rubric on page 82. Then complete the Partner Comments sheet that your teacher will give you. Tell what you like about the description and what you think would make it better.

9. **Switch** papers.

10. **Think about** your partner's comments. Read your essay again. Make changes that you think will improve your descriptive essay.

11. **Write** a neat final copy of your descriptive essay.

Making Connections

- As you read books and magazines and watch TV and movies, notice how sensory details are used to create vivid mental images. If used well, sensory details can make readers and viewers feel as if they are part of the story.

- Think about different ways you could order a description. If you were describing your room, you first might want to describe objects or areas that mean the most to you. This is called "order of importance." Think of other kinds of orders that you could use in your writing. How about orders based on location or size?

- Jot notes in your journal about people, places, or things that would be fun to describe. Remember that when you describe people, you can include details about how they behave. Does someone laugh, scratch his or her head, or sing a lot? What does he or she sing? Save your notes. They can provide ideas for future writing.

PERSONAL NARRATIVES

You tell stories all the time. Some are true, and some are invented. Some are about others, and some are about you.

A true story based on events in your own life is called a **personal narrative**.

Here is a sample writing prompt for a personal narrative.

> *Write about an experience that you will never forget.*

Read this personal narrative, which was written in response to the prompt. Then read the Writing Tips to learn more about personal narratives.

Writing Tips

❋ You can write about anything in your life, from a major turning point to an ordinary event.

❋ In a personal narrative, you write a true story about something that has happened in your life. Try to make readers part of your experience.

❋ Write as a first-person narrator. Use the first-person pronouns *I, me, we,* and *us* in your story.

❋ Put the story events in an order that makes sense. Make *sure* your story has a definite beginning, middle, and ending.

❋ Use transitional words such as *first, then,* and *next* to help readers follow the events.

❋ Use engaging, descriptive language that will *create* vivid images in the minds of your readers. For effect, you can occasionally use single phrases, such as "Mouse droppings!"

❋ If your personal narrative includes dialogue, make it realistic. If read out loud, your dialogue should sound like real people talking to each other. In your dialogue, use indentation, quotation marks, and other punctuation correctly.

❋ Create a story title that will capture readers' interest.

A Fright in the Night

It was my first camping trip. For weeks my family had planned it, and now we were in the Rockies. "We're here!" I announced to everyone.

The first day we hiked to a lake where we made camp. After supper we scoured our dishes with lake sand and warm water from the kettle. We wiped the picnic table and put our food in a pack, which we hoisted with a rope over a high tree branch. This was to keep prowling animals out of it.

We stirred the campfire coals and turned in early that night. We all fell asleep fast, side by side in the tent. Suddenly, I woke up. It was pitch dark, and something was out there! Whatever it was, it was nosing around, and it sounded clumsy. Something moved on the table, but what had we left out? I made a mental list. There were only clean dishes, salt and pepper, towels, and a plastic water container.

My mind raced. It must be a bear! Was it a grizzly? My body stiffened with terror as I pictured an enormous paw suddenly swiping the tent wall. Thin nylon was all that separated the four-inch claws from us. I don't know how long I lay frozen like that, but the noises seemed to go for hours.

Then it was dawn. Everyone else was still asleep, and the tent was still standing. I dressed and crawled out to examine the damage. The food pack still dangled from the branch, untouched. Only the salt shaker had moved, and it was tipped on its side. The intruder had left a single clue. Mouse droppings!

USING GRAPHIC ORGANIZERS

Before you write, use graphic organizers to help yourself gather and arrange the content for your story.

The writer of the personal narrative on page 86 might have used a Story Chart, such as the one below.

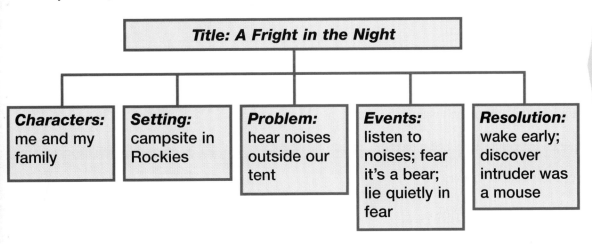

The writer of the story on page 86 might also have used a Setting Chart to organize information about the setting of the story. If you had been the writer, what details would you have used to describe the setting? Fill in the boxes on the chart below with details about three aspects of the setting.

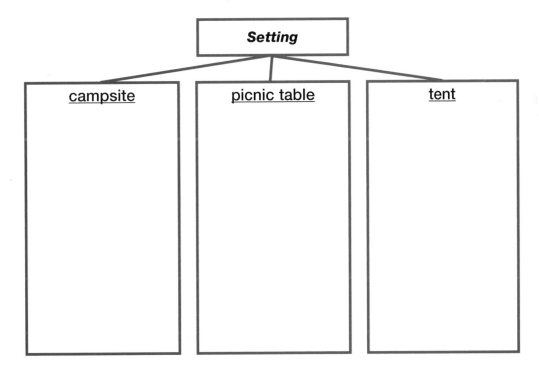

Score:

Read the personal narrative below, which was written in response to the prompt on page 86. Read the comments and think about why this story scored a 4.

Your Turn

Now it's your turn to help the writer. Find and fix the errors in the writing. Go back to the pages in green if you need help.

1. Find and fix the **capitalization** error in a name. See pp. 46–47.
2. Find and fix the missing **quotation marks**. See pp. 56–57.

Pianissimo

I'll never forget the worst recital of my life. It happened one summer night when I was eight.

"Time to go," Mother urged. "You don't want to be late."

They were waiting on the porch. They had turned the lights off. I was practicing my piece one last time, in the dark.

"You've got it down now," father coaxed.

Unconvinced, I followed them out to the car.

Soon I was cowering backstage. The concert hall, the stage, and the piano looked huge. The piano was the long, fancy style called a concert grand. With the top propped up, it loomed like an ugly black sailboat. Why hadn't my teacher told me? My hands started to sweat.

One by one, the other students played their pieces perfectly by heart. Then I heard myself announce, "Beethoven's 'Moonlight Sonata,' Second Movement."

I perched on the bench, steadied my fingers on the keys, and breathed. The melody began. Everything was going fine, but then a weird thing happened. It was like I was watching someone else's hands, and they were about to stop. My mind was going blank! I showed no reaction and started over, hoping the audience wouldn't notice. It happened again. I started again. Then, like a nightmare, it happened one more time! I stood up and curtseyed, but the audience clapped too long. They pitied me!

Later that night, I played the "Moonlight Sonata on our little piano with the plastic keys. No one heard but me, but I played it perfectly. I knew that I could!

TEACHER COMMENTS

▲ Your title is a foreign word and may be hard for some readers, but it gives a good hint about the story's focus.

▲ Your story has a consistent point, and it's clearly your own.

▲ The "ugly black sailboat" is an excellent image because it tells how the piano looked to you and how it made you feel. You invite readers in. Good!

▲ Your sentences are varied, clear, and complete. You've used correct punctuation and capitalization.

▲ Your story is well-structured, with a definite beginning, middle, and ending. Nice job!

PARTNER COMMENTS

Your story made me imagine your experience, as if it happened to me! The opening dialogue got my interest. The ending was good too.

Read the personal narrative and the comments that follow. Think about why this story scored a 3.

Play It Again, Kid

The worst night of my life was the night of my piano recital when I was eight. I remember my mom and dad waiting on the porch and telling me to hurry up so we wouldn't be late. I went on playing my piece in the dark one more time even after they had turned off the lights.

Then, when we got to the concert hall, it looked totally huge. The piano scared me half to death because it was the concert grand kind. I had never played on one like that before!

It seemed like all the other kids weren't even nervous. Then it was my turn. I was going to play Beethoven's Moonlight Sonata," the second part.

I remember being so nervous that my hands were sweating, and I wondered if I would even be able to press the keys down. Then I started playing but a totally weird thing happened. It was like I was not even playing myself. I sort of panicked because I thought I was going to forget the rest! I figured I could fake it, so I went on playing. I went back to the beginning, but I forgot two more times! Finally I had to get up and curtsey. The audience clapped as if they felt sorry for me. It was the worse feeling I had ever had!

Later that night, after everybody else had gone to bed, I stayed up and played my piece one more time just to see if I could and I did and with no mistakes. Even if it wasn't in front of the audience, it made me feel a lot better.

Your Turn

Now it's your turn to help the writer. Find and fix the errors in the writing. Go back to the pages in green if you need help.

1. Find and fix the **paragraph** that isn't indented. See pp. 58–59.
2. Find and fix the missing **quotation marks**. See pp. 56–57.
3. Find and fix the **compound sentence** that is missing a **comma**. See pp. 30–31.
4. Find and fix the incorrect **comparative** form of an **adjective**. See pp. 22–23.
5. Find and fix the **rambling sentence**. See pp. 40–41.

TEACHER COMMENTS 4

▲ Your title is clever. Nice!

▲ You have kept your own point of view and have presented some interesting story details. I can tell what you were thinking and feeling. Good!

▲ Though a story should sound like it is being told to a friend, some of your words are too informal. Use terms such as *totally* and *it was like* sparingly.

▲ Some of your sentences are long and sound rushed. You should vary your **sentence structure**. See pp. 44–45 for help.

▲ Try using some **words** that are more **exact** or **precise**. See pp. 4–5 and 22–27.

PARTNER COMMENTS 3 2

I could imagine the events and feelings in the story. The writing was kind of rambling, though. The ending was choppy.

Score:

(2)

Read the personal narrative and the comments that follow. Think about why this story scored a 2.

1

Blew It

I had to play piano in front of people one time. That was the worst thing I ever had to do. That was a bad night. I was seven or eight. I dont remember for sure. I hated that. It was because I was shy but they never asked if you wanted to or didn't want to but they just said do this and then you have to.

When we got their, the place was huge. I had never seen a piano like that before. It was a concert kind, and cost more than some houses! It was my turn. That was the first time I had played that kind of piano and it was not that easy, and now I know why. Those keys arent easy to press down, and there not plastic.

I forgot the end part of my music, but it was because those people are staring at me. You always play better when no one is there. I proved it later. The whole thing with no mistakes!

2

PARTNER COMMENTS

Your ideas moved around so much, I kept getting lost. I could tell that you had an awful experience, though.

Your Turn

Now it's your turn to help the writer. Find and fix the errors in the writing. Go back to the pages in green if you need help.

1. Find and fix the two **contraction** errors. See pp. 54–55.

2. Find and fix the two **rambling sentences**. See pp. 40–41.

3. Find and fix the two **inconsistent verb tenses**. See pp. 42–43.

4. Find and fix the **paragraph** that is not indented. See pp. 58–59.

5. Find and fix the two incorrect **homophones**. See pp. 28–29.

6. Find and fix the **comma** used incorrectly in a **simple sentence** with a **compound predicate**. See pp. 30–31 and 44–45.

7. Find and fix the **sentence fragment**. See pp. 34–35.

TEACHER COMMENTS

4

▲ Although your title is "catchy" and relates to the story, it is a slang expression. Think of another title.

▲ Your story details are often weak, so I have a hard time picturing the time, place, and events. I do know how you felt, though.

▲ Make sure you don't get off track with points that don't develop the story.

▲ Your sentences tend to be too long or too short. I'd like to see you vary the **structure** of some **sentences** and the **types** of **sentences** you use. See pp. 30–31, 36–37, and 44–45 for help.

▲ Use more precise **words**. See pp. 4–5 and 22–27.

▲ The ideas in your paragraphs run together. Make sure you create a new **paragraph** for each new idea. Remember to **indent**. See pp. 58–59.

3

Read the personal narrative and the comments that follow. Think about why this story scored a 1.

One time this girl had a teacher who sayed she had to play piano in front of all these people. That girl felt like running away that night her parents said she should do it, so she said she would. Then herself stood up and said that it was mr. beethovens "Moonlight Sonata. Then she got part way through and then forgot the rest. Three times. Like a nightmare. It makes me mad shy kids should not have to do this I will not ever make my kids do it. The girl played it by heart after everybody had went to bed. That didnt really count, but her and I know it did, and that is for sure.

PARTNER COMMENTS

2

Was this story about your life? It didn't seem to be. It didn't have a clear beginning, middle, and ending. You made a lot of errors that you should fix.

TEACHER COMMENTS

3

▲ Your story needs a title.

▲ The story should be told from your point of view. It isn't clear that you are describing your own experience. It sounds like you are telling a story about someone else. Are you?

▲ Take time to write more details so that your story will get and hold your readers' attention.

▲ Please vary your **sentence structure** and the **types of sentences** you use. See pp. 30–31, 36–37, and 44–45 for help.

▲ Please **join** some **short sentences** when they have related ideas. See pp. 36–37.

Your Turn

Now it's your turn to help the writer. Find and fix the errors in the writing. Go back to the pages in green if you need help.

1. Find and fix the two **verb tense** errors. See pp. 16–17.

2. Find and fix the two **run-on sentences.** See pp. 40–41.

3. Find and fix the two incorrect **pronouns.** See pp. 10–11 and 14–15.

4. Find and fix the two **capitalization** errors. See pp. 46–47.

5. Find and fix the incorrect **possessive noun.** See pp. 8–9.

6. Find and fix the missing **quotation marks.** See pp. 56–57.

7. Find and fix the two **sentence fragments.** See pp. 34–35.

8. Find and fix the **contraction** error. See pp. 54–55.

9. Find and fix the **unnecessary clause.** See pp. 42–43.

4

USING A RUBRIC TO SCORE PERSONAL NARRATIVES

This rubric is based on a point scale of 1 to 4. It was used to score the personal narratives on pages 88–91. Use the rubric to remember what is important in personal narratives.

4 A score of 4 means that the writer

- ❑ connects the writing directly to the prompt.
- ❑ almost always uses the correct forms of words.
- ❑ almost always uses capitalization and punctuation correctly.
- ❑ almost always uses clear and complete sentences and uses variety in sentences.
- ❑ uses precise words and effective transitional words to connect ideas.
- ❑ creates an attention-getting title that relates to the story.
- ❑ creates a clear beginning, middle, and ending.
- ❑ tells the story from his or her point of view and uses pronouns such as *I, me, we,* and *us.*
- ❑ provides many engaging story details, including thoughts and feelings.
- ❑ includes realistic dialogue.
- ❑ begins a new paragraph for each change of idea or speaker.

2 A score of 2 means that the writer

- ❑ connects the writing to the prompt in a general way.
- ❑ uses some incorrect forms of words.
- ❑ uses some incorrect capitalization or punctuation.
- ❑ uses little variety in sentences.
- ❑ uses some run-on or rambling sentences or sentence fragments.
- ❑ uses mostly simple words and few transitional words.
- ❑ creates a title that relates somewhat to the story.
- ❑ creates a weak beginning, middle, or ending.
- ❑ usually tells the story from his or her point of view but may not seem connected to the story.
- ❑ provides few effective story details.
- ❑ includes little or no dialogue.
- ❑ may make some paragraphing errors.

3 A score of 3 means that the writer

- ❑ connects the writing to the prompt.
- ❑ usually uses the correct forms of words.
- ❑ usually uses capitalization and punctuation correctly.
- ❑ usually uses clear and complete sentences and uses some variety in sentences.
- ❑ uses some precise words and some transitional words.
- ❑ creates a title that relates generally to the story.
- ❑ creates a beginning, middle, and ending.
- ❑ tells the story from his or her point of view.
- ❑ provides some effective story details, including thoughts and feelings.
- ❑ includes dialogue.
- ❑ usually begins a new paragraph for each change of idea or speaker.

1 A score of 1 means that the writer

- ❑ does not successfully connect the writing to the prompt.
- ❑ uses many incorrect forms of words.
- ❑ often uses incorrect capitalization or punctuation.
- ❑ uses almost no variety in sentences.
- ❑ uses many run-on or rambling sentences or sentence fragments.
- ❑ uses simple or inappropriate words and very few transitional words.
- ❑ creates a weak title or has no title at all.
- ❑ creates an unclear beginning, middle, or ending.
- ❑ doesn't tell the story from his or her point of view or switches point of view.
- ❑ provides weak or confusing story details.
- ❑ does not use dialogue or uses it incorrectly.
- ❑ may make many paragraphing errors.

SCORING PERSONAL NARRATIVES

Now it's your turn to score some personal narratives. The four stories on pages 93 and 94 were written in response to this prompt.

> *Write about an embarrassing moment that you have had.*

Read each personal narrative. Write a few comments about it. Then give it a score from 1 to 4. Think about what you've learned in this lesson as you match each story with its correct score.

Model A

Score:

My most embarrassing moment was when I took a tennis test. I had taken some tennis lessons but I wasn't very good. I didn't know if I would pass the final test.

When the test time came my teacher said to hit the ball over a white line on the backboard. He would count how many times I hit it over the line in a minute. I tried to picture myself hitting it over the line but I couldn't really picture it.

I did hit the ball one time over the line, but it went high and sailed over the fence! Now what? I chased it, but my teacher said that I was the worse player he had ever seen. He was really rude, but he was probably right.

Comments: _____

_____

_____

_____

_____

_____

_____

Model B

Score:

Some people hates sports and its really true when they dont play good. No matter how they try they cant hit to save theyselves. Im not as bad as that but I'm not all that good not like my cousin, that guy is real good. He will play anything long as you give him a ball to hit. One time I taked tennis lessons trying to learn but come time for the test I lookd pretty bad. The Teacher sayed I was not to good, in fact you will not pass! But win some lose some, like they say.

Comments: _____

_____

_____

_____

_____

_____

_____

Model C

Score:

No Pro

I've never been an athlete, but I wanted to play tennis, so I took some lessons. Unfortunately, I never got any good. Whenever I saw the ball flying toward me, I'd get out of the way! That's why I was worried about the test at the end of the course.

When the dreaded day arrived, my teacher was waiting with a stopwatch. He said, "Okay, let's see how many times you can hit the ball over that white line on the backboard. Ready? Go!" His thumb pressed the top of the watch.

I tossed a ball up, swung the racket, and sent the ball above the waist-high line. Actually, I sent it to the top of the backboard, where it flew off into the sky. What should I do? I raced after it!

When I came back with the ball, my teacher shook his head and said, "Your score is one. Your the worse tennis player I have ever seen! That was mean, but he had a point. I have not played tennis since then.

Comments: _____
_____
_____
_____
_____
_____
_____
_____

Model D

Score:

Never again

I remember one time when I took a tennis test. I was a real bad player. I took some lessons but they didn't help. I guess I was not very good at sports in general but at least I tried.

The bad moment was when it come time for the test I had to hit the ball over the line. The teacher was timing me. I hit the ball, it hit the board. Then flew off over the fence. I ran off to get it but too late. The teacher said that was the worse tennis he ever saw. The end!

Comments: _____
_____
_____
_____
_____
_____
_____
_____

WRITING A PERSONAL NARRATIVE

Now you get to write your own personal narrative. Use the prompt below.

> *Write about a time when you made an important discovery.*

When You Write Your Personal Narrative

1. **Think about** what you want to write. Ask yourself some questions.
   - What are the key story events?
   - Where and when did the events take place?
   - As the narrator, what tone do I want to use?
   - Who else besides me belongs in the story?
   - How will I begin the story?
   - How will I end the story?

   Use graphic organizers to gather and sort the information.

2. **Write** your first draft. Write down all the important events and details.

3. **Read** your draft. Use the checklist that your teacher will give you to review your writing.

4. **Edit** your story. Make changes until your story reads well.

5. **Proofread** your personal narrative one last time.

6. **Write** a neat copy of your personal narrative and give it to your partner.

Work with a Partner

7. **Read** your partner's personal narrative.

8. **Score** your partner's story from 1 to 4, using the rubric on page 92. Then complete the Partner Comments sheet that your teacher will give you. Tell what you like about the story and what you think would make it better.

9. **Switch** papers.

10. **Think about** your partner's comments. Read your story again. Make changes that you think will improve your personal narrative.

11. **Write** a neat final copy of your personal narrative.

Making Connections

- In your journal, jot down ideas about things you have seen or done recently. Did something unusual happen on the bus today? Did you find or lose something, overhear a fascinating story, or make a wish? Your notes may become ideas for future personal narratives.

- Practice writing personal narratives as letters to friends. See how you can turn ordinary or amusing events or experiences into stories that share your ideas and feelings.

- Make a life graph of your life experiences. Use it to generate ideas for stories you would like to tell. You can use these story ideas as prompts for writing future personal narratives. Consider submitting one to a school newspaper, magazine, or website.

FICTIONAL NARRATIVES

A fictional narrative is a story that is not true. It comes from your imagination and is usually about characters and events that you invent. Here is a sample writing prompt for a fictional narrative.

> *Write a story about a character who experiences something unexpected.*

Read the fictional narrative, which was written in response to the prompt. Then read the Writing Tips to learn more about fictional narratives.

Writing Tips

These elements are important in fictional narratives.

Story Structure

The title should make readers want to read the story.

Beginning

❉ Setting: the time and place of the story

❉ Characters: the people in the story, consisting of a main character and one or more supporting characters

❉ Problem or Conflict: a situation, question, or goal that the characters must deal with

Middle

❉ Plot Events: events that make up the action of the story, presented in a logical order, showing how the characters deal with the problem

❉ Climax: the high point or turning point in the plot events

Ending

❉ Resolution: how the characters have dealt with, or accepted, the problem

❉ Outcome: the very end of the story, where loose ends are tied up

Narrator: the "voice" or narrative point of view of the story. A first-person narrator is part of the story. A third-person narrator is separate from the story and tells what happens to others.

Dialogue: what the characters say to each other; builds characters and adds realism

Imagery: descriptive details, sensory words, and comparisons used to make the story come alive

---

The Misfit

Elsbeth had moved to Cleveland just in time to start the school year. Now she was worried. What if she didn't fit in? She had been living in Mexico and didn't always dress like the other girls.

When her teacher assigned her the last seat in the row, Elsbeth was glad. Sitting in back, she could be practically invisible. But one day she had to walk to the front to hand in a paper. Elsbeth hesitated. That morning she had worn her *gaban*, a poncho woven with bright pink and red yarns. Did it make her stand out too much?

As Elsbeth passed Rex, she heard him hiss, "What is *that*?" She turned and saw him laughing behind her back.

That night, Elsbeth placed the *gaban* gently in the bottom drawer of her dresser. She was more angry than hurt. What did Rex know? The bright colors blurred. She *would* wear it again!

On Monday, Elsbeth strolled home from the bus stop with Ann, a girl in her class. She invited Ann in for a snack. They were in the kitchen when Ann asked to see the *gaban*.

"Why?" Elsbeth asked, startled.

"I never got a good look at it. I would like to see the weaving up close." Ann added, "I'm a little jealous."

"Jealous?" Now Elsbeth was amazed.

"Sure," Ann said. "No one else has anything like that."

The next day, Rex had to look twice. There was the *gaban* again, but this time it was on Ann! By November, every girl in class had borrowed it. Elsbeth had made new friends, and she had started a fad!

USING GRAPHIC ORGANIZERS

Before you write, use graphic organizers to plan the content of your story.

The writer of the fictional narrative on page 96 might have used a Character Cluster such as the one below.

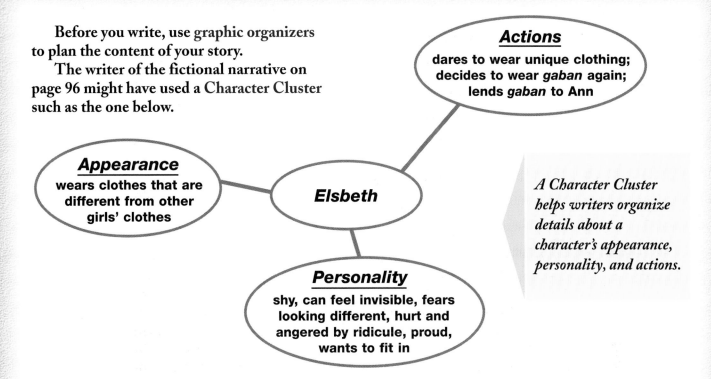

Actions
dares to wear unique clothing; decides to wear *gaban* again; lends *gaban* to Ann

Appearance
wears clothes that are different from other girls' clothes

Elsbeth

Personality
shy, can feel invisible, fears looking different, hurt and angered by ridicule, proud, wants to fit in

A Character Cluster helps writers organize details about a character's appearance, personality, and actions.

The writer of the story on page 96 might also have used a Story Diagram such as the one below to plan the story's action. If you were the writer, how would you complete the diagram? The Climax is filled in. Complete the rest of the diagram.

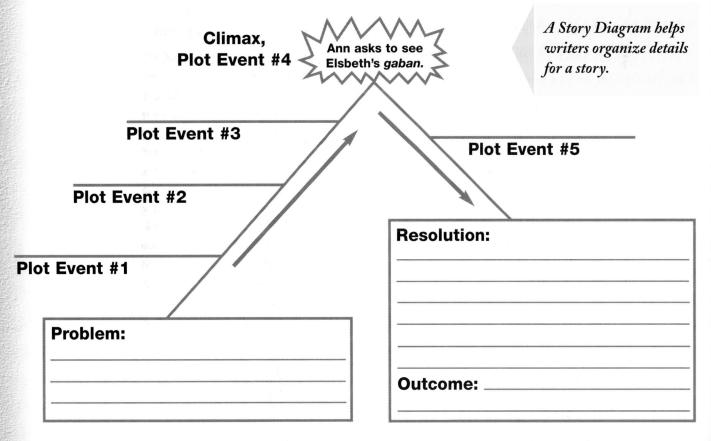

A Story Diagram helps writers organize details for a story.

Climax, Plot Event #4
Ann asks to see Elsbeth's *gaban*.

Plot Event #3

Plot Event #5

Plot Event #2

Plot Event #1

Resolution:

Problem:

Outcome:

Score: 4

Read the fictional narrative below, which was written in response to the prompt on page 96. Read the comments and think about why this story scored a 4.

The Mysterious Light

Late one August night, the Woo family was driving home after visiting the Wangs' ranch. Doug Woo had spent time with the sheep and with Zack, the collie. He had watched the fish in Mr. Wang's aquarium.

As the car sped on, Dad turned the radio on low. Moms eyes closed. Nell dozed beside Doug in the back seat, clutching her bear, Lou. Dreamily, Doug watched the dark trees whizzing by. Maybe he'd become a veterinarian someday. His mind replayed images from the day: the fleecy sheep, the colorful fish, and big, gentle Zack. Just then, a ball of light flashed where Doug was staring, glided past, and was gone.

"Dad!" Doug shouted.

"What was that?" Dad exclaimed.

They compared what they'd seen. They agreed that the light was the size of a soccer ball. It had a bright violet core. It had traveled parallel to the road, in a straight line, as high as a telephone pole. It had flown too low for a plane and too fast for an owl. It couldn't have been the moon or a comet. It must have been a spaceship!

Mom laughed. "This family had been watching too much TV."

"I didn't see anything," Nell said.

"You were unconscious!" Doug said.

Later, while surfing the Internet, Doug discovered a website about a natural event called a "lower atmospheric magnetoplasmoid," or ball lightning. This was the mysterious light. "Wow!" Doug said aloud. "Now I want to be a vet and a scientist!"

Your Turn

Now it's your turn to help the writer. Find and fix the errors in the writing. Go back to the pages in green if you need help.

1. Find and fix the incorrect **possessive noun**. See pp. 8–9.
2. Find and fix **verb** that should be in the **present perfect tense**. See pp. 16–17.

TEACHER COMMENTS

4

▲ Your title is a grabber, and you followed the prompt well.

▲ You quickly established a clear setting.

▲ The events in your story are active and engaging. You tell the story consistently from the third-person point of view. Thanks!

▲ You have chosen your words carefully. Your sentences are varied, and you use paragraphs correctly and effectively.

▲ Your story's characters and their dialogue seem realistic.

▲ The story resolves and concludes nicely from the climax, when Doug is surfing the Internet and finds the website. Well done!

PARTNER COMMENTS

3

2

I liked this story because I believed in the characters. The dialogue was realistic. The plot made sense.

Read the fictional narrative and the comments that follow. Think about why this story scored a 3.

1

The Mystery of the Bright Light

One night the Woo family was traveling home after visiting the Wangs, who owned a sheep ranch. Doug Woo had really enjoyed the day. He wanted to be a veterinarian, so the hole way home he kept picturing the Wangs sheep, their dog, and even the fish in there aquarium.

Everyone was sleepy in the car. Doug was gazing out the window when suddenly he saw a round flash of light. It was the most brightest that a light can be. It flew along in a straight line for about a second. Then it vanished. It didn't look like a plane, a bird, a train light, or anything else that Doug recognized.

"Dad did you see that?" Doug asked.

"Was it a spaceship?" his father asked.

"I don't know," Doug answers.

A long time later, Doug found an explanation for the mysterious light. He was using the Internet when he discovered a science web site that talked about lightning. What they had seen was something called "ball lightning."

Doug thought that discovering this is very exciting. Could he become a vet *and* a scientist?

Your Turn

Now it's your turn to help the writer. Find and fix the errors in the writing. Go back to the pages in green if you need help.

1. Find and fix the two incorrect **homophones**. See pp. 28–29.

2. Find and fix the incorrect **possessive noun**. See pp. 8–9.

3. Find and fix the **double comparison**. See pp. 22–23.

4. Find and fix the missing **comma** with a noun of **direct address**. See pp. 52–53.

5. Find and fix the two **inconsistent verb tenses**. See pp. 42–43.

TEACHER COMMENTS

4

▲ Your story has effective elements: setting, characters, and plot. Good.

▲ The action and dialogue are realistic. In some places, though, you could use better details. For example, did Doug press his face to the window when he saw the light?

▲ In the second paragraph, you should use more **sentence variety**. See pp. 44–45 for help.

▲ Doug's character is convincing. As a reader, I can understand his point of view from the beginning. Nicely done.

PARTNER COMMENTS

3

2

This story got me interested, but it could have had more dialogue. The writer could have told more about how the family felt about the unexpected light.

Score:

②

Read the fictional narrative and the comments that follow.
Think about why this story scored a 2.

What They Saw Driving Home

The Woos and the Wangs were friends. One night the Woos were on the way home from their friends ranch. Doug woo liked visiting the Wangs ranch to see their sheep. Their dog Zack and their fish.

Doug was half asleep in the back seat when it happened. He was looking out the window. His Dad was driving, but his mom had her eyes closed and so did his little sister and she was holding onto her stuffed bear.

All of a sudden there is a ball of light. It was bright. It is flying through the air. Doug said, "That is strange." They didn't no what it was. Later Doug found out it was something called "ball lightning."

Your Turn

Now it's your turn to help the writer. Find and fix the errors in the writing. Go back to the pages in green if you need help.

1. Find and fix the two incorrect **possessive nouns**. See pp. 8–9.
2. Find and fix the two **capitalization** errors. See pp. 46–47.
3. Find and fix the **sentence fragment**. See pp. 34–35.
4. Find and fix the two **paragraphs** that should be indented. See pp. 58–59.
5. Find and fix the **rambling sentence**. See pp. 40–41.
6. Find and fix the two **inconsistent verb tenses**. See pp. 42–43.
7. Find and fix the incorrect **homophone**. See pp. 28–29.

PARTNER COMMENTS

I had trouble understanding some of the plot. For example, why did Doug like seeing the animals on the ranch? How did the Woos feel about the light?

TEACHER COMMENTS

▲ Try to create a title that gives a better hint about what's to come in your story.

▲ Your story does have a beginning, middle, and ending, but everything seems rushed. Take time to tell your story, as if you were telling it to a friend.

▲ If you provided more information about the characters, setting, and plot events, readers could understand the story better and get more involved in it. More **dialogue** would make your characters seem more like real people. See pp. 56–57 for help.

▲ You could use more **sensory words** to add imagery to your story. See 58–59.

▲ I'd like to see more **variety** in your **sentences**. See pp. 30–31, 36–37, and 44–45.

Score: **1**

Read the fictional narrative and the comments that follow. Think about why this story scored a 1.

1

The Woos had visited they're friends the Wangs at the Wangs ranch. The Woos was in the car they were tired they was feeling kind of sleepy. Then all of a sudden their was this bright light. They couldnt figure it out. They asked what it was. They thought they had saw something from Space. Some kind of Lightning in a ball or something. It must have been scary.

2

PARTNER COMMENTS

What is the title? This is too short for a story. It doesn't even have a main character. I couldn't picture anything in my mind. It was too choppy to follow.

3

TEACHER COMMENTS

▲ Think of a good title for your story so that you can make your readers want to know more.

▲ Your story lacks a solid beginning, middle, and ending. Also, you change from third-person point of view to first-person point of view in the last sentence.

▲ You should have some specific characters, not just the Woo family and the Wang family. **Dialogue** would make the characters more believable. *See pp. 56–57 for help.*

▲ Take time to develop the setting and the story events. The action should build up and then be resolved.

▲ If you use more **interesting words**, your story would create a better picture in readers' minds. *See pp. 4–5 and 22–27.*

▲ Try to use more variety in the **structure** and **type** of **sentences** you use. *See pp. 30–31, 36–37, and 44–45.*

4

Your Turn

Now it's your turn to help the writer. Find and fix the errors in the writing. Go back to the pages in green if you need help.

1. Indent the **paragraph**. See pp. 58–59.

2. Find and fix the two incorrect **homophones**. See pp. 28–29.

3. Find and fix the incorrect **possessive noun**. See pp. 8–9.

4. Find and fix the **run-on sentence**. See pp. 40–41.

5. Find and fix the two errors in **subject-verb agreement**. See pp. 18–19.

6. Find and fix the **contraction** that is missing an **apostrophe**. See pp. 54–55.

7. Find and fix the error in **verb tense**. See pp. 16–17.

8. Find and fix the two **capitalization** errors. See pp. 48–51.

9. Find and fix the **sentence fragment**. See pp. 34–35.

USING A RUBRIC TO SCORE FICTIONAL NARRATIVES

This rubric is based on a point scale of 1 to 4. It was used to score the fictional narratives on pages 98–101. Use this rubric to remember what is important in fictional narratives.

4 A score of *4* means that the writer

- ❏ connects the writing directly to the prompt.
- ❏ almost always uses the correct forms of words.
- ❏ almost always uses capitalization and punctuation correctly.
- ❏ almost always uses clear and complete sentences and uses variety in sentences.
- ❏ creates an attention-getting title that relates to the story.
- ❏ uses many interesting words and details.
- ❏ creates a clear beginning, middle, and ending.
- ❏ develops a clear setting, one or more interesting characters, and an active plot with a problem, climax, resolution, and conclusion.
- ❏ uses realistic dialogue to make the characters come alive.
- ❏ uses a consistent narrative point of view.
- ❏ begins a new paragraph for each change of idea or speaker.

2 A score of *2* means that the writer

- ❏ connects the writing to the prompt in a general way.
- ❏ uses some incorrect forms of words.
- ❏ uses some incorrect capitalization or punctuation.
- ❏ uses little variety in sentences.
- ❏ uses some run-on or rambling sentences or sentence fragments.
- ❏ creates a title that relates somewhat to the story.
- ❏ uses mostly simple words and details.
- ❏ creates a weak beginning, middle, or ending.
- ❏ fails to clearly develop setting, characters, or plot.
- ❏ uses little or no dialogue.
- ❏ sometimes switches the narrative point of view.
- ❏ may make some paragraphing errors.

3 A score of *3* means that the writer

- ❏ connects the writing to the prompt.
- ❏ usually uses the correct forms of words.
- ❏ usually uses capitalization and punctuation correctly.
- ❏ usually uses clear and complete sentences and uses variety in sentences.
- ❏ creates a title that relates generally to the story.
- ❏ uses some interesting words and details.
- ❏ creates a beginning, middle, and ending.
- ❏ develops a setting, one or more characters, and a plot.
- ❏ uses some dialogue between characters.
- ❏ usually creates a consistent narrative point of view.
- ❏ usually begins a new paragraph for each change of idea or speaker.

1 A score of *1* means that the writer

- ❏ does not successfully connect the writing to the prompt.
- ❏ uses many incorrect forms of words.
- ❏ often uses incorrect capitalization or punctuation.
- ❏ uses almost no variety in sentences.
- ❏ uses several run-on or rambling sentences or sentence fragments.
- ❏ creates a poor title or has no title at all.
- ❏ uses very simple words and details.
- ❏ creates an unclear beginning, middle, or ending.
- ❏ fails to present or develop setting, characters, or plot.
- ❏ does not use dialogue or uses it incorrectly.
- ❏ often switches the narrative point of view.
- ❏ may make many paragraphing errors.

SCORING FICTIONAL NARRATIVES

Now it's your turn to score some fictional narratives. The four stories on pages 103 and 104 were written in response to this prompt.

> *Write a fictional narrative about a character who does something silly.*

Read each fictional narrative. Write a few comments about it. Then give it a score from 1 to 4. Think about what you've learned in this lesson as you match each story with its correct score.

Model A

Score:

Tumble Down Jill

Jills paper was going to be late. She went to the library and ran into her teacher after she had just gotten an enormous stack of books. She plopped down on a chair with the books.

"Hi Mrs. McAllister," she said.

"Hello," her teacher said.

"I'm doing research, she said. Jill went on talking, but she wasn't very steady on the chair. While she was talking she started to tip. Her teacher stared with a worried look on her face, and she slid off of her chair, books and all. Jills teacher never forgot that day!

Comments: _____

_____

_____

_____

_____

_____

_____

_____

Model B

Score:

Not too Cool

Whom was it that wrote the song "Its now or never." Elvis the king. Well once there was this girl named Jill who wanted to make her teacher think she was smart. But she didn't ever notice her, actually she just never spoke up. So one day she had a plan but made totally a fool of herself when she tried to impress her. It was at the library and the girl had tons of books and sat on a chair and she slipped off of her chair and they all fell and that was that.

Comments: _____

_____

_____

_____

_____

_____

_____

_____

Model C

Score:

Jill was a girl who all she ever done is start her paper late and why she never speak up in class in the first place Ill never know. Probably to shy. Then she was putting her paper off so she goes to the library and she has it all planned what to do to get the teachers eye. She comes in and Jill says, "Hi." She sits down and then falls with the books all over! Hair brush, lipstick, glasses too. Sure got that teachers Eye, I can tell you!

Comments: _____

_____

_____

_____

_____

_____

_____

Model D

Score:

The Chance

Jill was getting nervous. She hadn't picked a topic for her paper, and it was due on Friday. On Tuesday, Jill raced to the library. Staggering out of the stacks with thirteen books, she spied her teacher at a table. This was her chance to prove she was no dummy!

"Hi Mrs. McAllister," Jill whispered.

"Hello Jill," Mrs. McAllister said.

"My research," Jill said, nodding to her books and reaching with one foot to pull out a chair. Mrs. McAllister raised an eyebrow. It was working! Jill perched awkwardly on the chair, with the tower of books on her lap.

"My topic . . . ," she began, trying to balance. It wasn't working. Jill kept talking as the chair tipped and she slowly slid off, spilling the books and everything in her pack all over the floor.

Jill's paper was on time, but she wasn't sure how smart Mrs. McAllister thought she was!

Comments: _____

_____

_____

_____

_____

_____

_____

WRITING A FICTIONAL NARRATIVE

Now you get to write your own fictional narrative. Use the prompt below.

> *Write a fictional narrative about a character who has to make a choice.*

When You Write Your Fictional Narrative

1. **Think about** what you want to write. Ask yourself some questions.
   - Where and when will the story take place?
   - Who will be in the story?
   - What problem will the characters have to deal with?
   - What will be the turning point in the action?
   - How will the problem be resolved?
   - How will the story end?

   Use graphic organizers to gather and sort the information.

2. **Write** your first draft. Be sure your story has a clear beginning, middle, and ending. Keep the narrative point of view consistent.

3. **Read** your draft. Use the checklist that your teacher will give you to review your writing.

4. **Edit** your story. Make changes until the setting and characters are clear and strong and the plot makes sense and is easy to follow.

5. **Proofread** your fictional narrative one last time.

6. **Write** a neat copy of your fictional narrative and give it to your partner.

Work with a Partner

7. **Read** your partner's story.

8. **Score** your partner's story from 1 to 4, using the rubric on page 102. Then complete the Partner Comments sheet that your teacher will give you. Tell what you like about the story and what you think would make it better.

9. **Switch** papers.

10. **Think about** your partner's comments. Read your story again. Make changes that you think will improve your fictional narrative.

11. **Write** a neat final copy of your fictional narrative.

Making Connections

- Think about the stories that you enjoy telling over and over again. Make a list of them. Pick a story and write it with the same tone you would use if you were telling it aloud to a friend.

- Keep a journal in which you jot down story ideas based on ordinary things in the world around you. Your notes may give you ideas for characters, settings, events, or entire plots of fictional stories that you can write about at a future time.

- Fantasy fiction stories often take place in make-believe settings and may include imaginary elements such as flying books, talking trees, and futuristic beam machines. Jot ideas for fantasy fiction stories in your journal as you think of them.

- When you watch a movie or TV show, notice which characters you react to strongly. Analyze why you do. How is your response affected by the way a character talks, moves, dresses, or behaves? Think about your reactions when you create your own story characters.

EXPOSITORY ESSAYS

An expository essay is a short paper that explains something. The information that you present in an expository essay often comes from what you already know about the topic.

Here is a sample writing prompt for an expository essay.

> *Write an essay explaining how to do something.*

Read this expository essay, which was written in response to the prompt. Then read the Writing Tips to learn more about expository essays.

Writing Tips

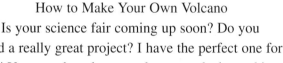

* Capture your readers' interest right away. Think of an interesting and relevant title. Make readers want to read on.

* Your introductory paragraph should tell what the essay is about in a clear topic sentence that relates to the whole essay, not just to the first paragraph. You may also capture readers' interest with an engaging detail, a thought-provoking question, or some interesting background information.

* The main purpose of your essay is to explain. The middle, or body, of your essay should include at least three main ideas about the essay topic, along with facts, examples, or reasons that develop the main ideas. Devote a paragraph to each main idea and remember to indent.

* The details that you provide may sometimes come from reference books and other sources, but they will often come from your own life experiences or observations. You can express a few opinions in the essay, but you should stick mainly to facts.

* Present your main ideas in a logical order, using appropriate transitional words and phrases to help one idea move smoothly into the next.

* Create a closing paragraph that gives readers a sense of conclusion. Do this by summing up the main ideas, restating the topic sentence in a different way, or giving an overview or a final thought about the topic. Do not introduce any new information in the conclusion.

How to Make Your Own Volcano

Is your science fair coming up soon? Do you need a really great project? I have the perfect one for you! You can show how a volcano works by making your own volcano. It's really quite easy.

First, you'll want to make sure you have all the necessary supplies. Here's what you'll need: a shallow pan, some natural-looking colors of modeling clay, a small cap from a spray can, $\frac{1}{4}$ cup of water, 1 tablespoon of baking soda, a few drops of red food coloring, a few drops of liquid dishwashing soap, and $\frac{1}{4}$ cup of vinegar.

Once you've gathered everything together, put the pan on a table covered with newspapers. Use brown modeling clay to form the tip of the volcano around the spray-can cap. Then use red or yellow clay to build the base of the volcano, with lava flowing down the sides. To add a finishing touch, put some green clay at the bottom for grass.

Then scoop out a hole in the tip of the volcano. After you mix the baking soda, red food coloring, and dishwashing soap into the water, pour it into the cap through the hole at the tip of the volcano. When the judge comes around to score your project, pour the vinegar into the hole. Then watch everyone's eyes pop as the volcano begins to erupt!

This experiment is not only fun, but it also proves what happens when you combine baking soda and an acid, vinegar.

Use graphic organizers to plan and organize the content of your essay.

The writer of the expository essay on page 106 might have used a Flowchart such as the one below to organize the steps in making a volcano.

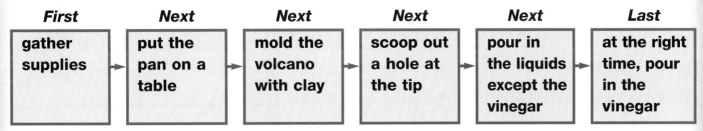

First	Next	Next	Next	Next	Last
gather supplies	put the pan on a table	mold the volcano with clay	scoop out a hole at the tip	pour in the liquids except the vinegar	at the right time, pour in the vinegar

A Flowchart helps writers plan the order of steps, first to last, that make up a "how to" expository essay.

The writer of the essay on page 106 might also have used a Main Ideas/Details Chart, such as the one below. If you were the writer, how might you have used this chart to organize the main ideas and supporting details? Fill in the details next to each main idea.

A Main Ideas/Details Chart helps writers organize information for an essay.

Main Ideas	Details
• Gather the Supplies	_____
	_____
	_____
	_____
	_____
• Mold the Volcano	_____
	_____
• Mix All Ingredients Except Vinegar	_____
	_____
• Add the Vinegar	_____
	_____

Score:
4

Read the expository essay below, which was written in response to the prompt on page 106. Read the comments and think about why this essay scored a 4.

1

Earthquake Planning Counts!

Earthquakes happen all over the world, yet people are often not prepared for them when they strike. For that reason, you and your family should make an earthquake plan. It could protect you, your pets, and your belongings.

The first step is to find the safest spot in every room of your home. It might be in a hallway, against an inner wall, or under a sturdy table or desk.

The second step is to locate the most dangerous spots. This means identifying objects that could break or fall during an earthquake. Look at windows, mirrors, hanging pictures or lamps, tall furniture, heavy appliances, or bookshelves. Work with your family to make these items more secure.

Next, put together a first-aid kit, a few days supply of canned or dried food, several gallons of water, a flashlight, a radio, batteries, blankets, and extra clothes. If an earthquake is severe it could leave you and your family trapped without water, gas, or electricity. Have older family members locate the valves for gas and water. If the lines get damaged, these valves will have to be turned off. Also make a list of emergency phone numbers.

Finally, have an emergency earthquake drill. With your family, identify all the safe ways to evacuate your home in case that becomes necessary. Practice each way, remembering that some ways may become blocked during a quake.

You may never experience a major earthquake. If you've made an earthquake plan though, you'll be prepared.

Your Turn

Now it's your turn to help the writer. Find and fix the errors in the writing. Go back to the pages in green if you need help.

1. Find and fix the incorrect **possessive noun**. See pp. 8–9.
2. Find and fix the missing **comma** with an **introductory dependent clause**. See pp. 52–53.

TEACHER COMMENTS

4

▲ Your introductory paragraph presents a strong topic sentence and gives readers good reason to want to know more about how to plan for an earthquake.

▲ Your essay is logically ordered by steps, with transitional words. You provide many details that develop each step.

▲ Your sentences are clear, complete, and varied.

▲ Your words are well chosen and informative.

▲ The last paragraph, and especially the last sentence, concludes the essay very nicely.

3
PARTNER COMMENTS

2

This was a really good essay. I learned a lot. You organized the information well and gave plenty of details.

Read the expository essay and the comments that follow. Think about why this essay scored a 3.

1

Don't Get Shaken Up

Planning for emergencies is always a good idea. It could save your life and it could protect your family and things. That's why making an earthquake plan is a smart thing to do.

You should start by figuring out where the safe places are. In the whole house, not just your room. You should also check to see if there are any things that aren't stationery and that could hurt people if they fell. Look for heavy mirrors or pictures or furniture.

Another thing to do is to have an emergency drill to practice getting out of the house in case you have to. Don't forget that the ways that you usually go in and out might be blocked if the building gets shaken up. It can be a hole different world!

You should always keep a first-aid kit. It might come in handy. You should also have other supplies, just in case. A box with food, water, and flashlights are good to have. You don't want to be trapped with nothing to eat. Another danger is that the gas lines could break. If that happens, do not light a match. That could cause an explosion. Even if you are careful.

At night with an earthquake preparation plan, you will sleep better.

Your Turn

Now it's your turn to help the writer. Find and fix the errors in the writing. Go back to the pages in green if you need help.

1. Find and fix **compound sentence** that is missing a **comma**. See pp. 30–31.
2. Find and fix the two **sentence fragments**. See pp. 34–35.
3. Find and fix the two incorrect **homophones**. See pp. 28–29.
4. Find and fix the error in **subject-verb agreement**. See pp. 18–19.
5. Find and fix the **misplaced modifier**. See pp. 32–33.

TEACHER COMMENTS

4

▲ Your title is catchy, but it would be better if you could include the word earthquakes.

▲ Your opening paragraph introduces the topic right away. Thank you.

▲ In the middle of your essay, you have plenty of main ideas. However, I'd like to see more supporting details.

▲ Try to vary the **kinds of sentences** you use. See pp. 30–31 and 44–45 for help.

2

PARTNER COMMENTS

3

Your essay was well organized. It explained enough that I could understand what you were saying. I will make a plan myself.

Score:
2

Read the expository essay and the comments that follow. Think about why this essay scored a 2.

1

The Earthquake

This essay is about earthquakes. They can be real scary. They can shake up a building, break the windows, knock stuff off the shelves, crack the mirror, bust the TV, and start a fire!

You might be minding your own business, all of a sudden one hits. What if your in bed? You won't know what to do. What if you are in the kitchen and the refrigerator starts rolling toward you? Thats not funny even if it sounds funny.

That is why you need an earthquake plan. You should practice how to get out. Just in case you have to. It is more easier to get out when you practice. You wont panic.

Also there are safe places in your house you should find where they were because you do not want to be looking around later.

Now you no about earthquakes.

Your Turn

Now it's your turn to help the writer. Find and fix the errors in the writing. Go back to the pages in green if you need help.

1. Find and fix the **adjective** that should be an **adverb**. See pp. 26–27.
2. Find and fix the two **run-on sentences**. See pp. 40–41.
3. Find and fix the two incorrect **homophones**. See pp. 28–29.
4. Find and fix the two **contractions** that are missing an **apostrophe**. See pp. 54–55.
5. Find and fix the **sentence fragment**. See 34–35.
6. Find and fix the **double comparison**. See pp. 22–23.
7. Find and fix the **inconsistent verb tense**. See pp. 42–43.

2

PARTNER COMMENTS

3

You didn't follow the prompt. You didn't explain how to make the earthquake plan. You gave some good warnings, though.

TEACHER COMMENTS

4

▲ You were supposed to write about how to do something, not about the thing itself. You don't mention the "how to" plan until the third paragraph.

▲ To explain the plan adequately, you need to include at least three **main ideas along with supporting details**. You present a lot of reasons for having a plan, but you don't give enough specifics about the plan. *See pp. 58–59 for help.*

▲ Each paragraph should have a **lead** and **transitional words** or **phrases** that guide readers into the main idea. *See pp. 60–61.*

▲ Your image about the refrigerator rolling away is effective. Try for better **word choices** in the rest of your essay. *See pp. 4–5 and 22–27.*

▲ You should use your last paragraph to wrap up the ideas about the earthquake plan.

Read the expository essay and the comments that follow. Think about why this essay scored a 1.

I was in an earthquake once, I no they are scary. I had just went to sleep. Then the door slammed. The lamp by my bed starts wobbling. I jumped up just in time to keep it from hitting me in the head and knocking me out. My Brother would have called me dumb.

"Get me out of here! If you make a plan, though. You wont be stuck like that. It is a good idea. Right some notes.

Look around your house. If you want my opinion. It is not that hard. Just do it in case their is an earthquake. Thats all.

PARTNER COMMENTS

You didn't follow the prompt. Your essay was more like a story. You should have told how to do something.

TEACHER COMMENTS

▲ Your essay needs a title.

▲ Although your opening sentence will get readers' attention, it doesn't indicate that you will explain how to do something.

▲ Your essay needs to develop a "how to" topic with several **main ideas** and **supporting details**. See pp. 58–59 for help.

▲ You need to pay more attention to **word choices**. See pp. 4–5 and 22–27.

▲ Vary the **structure** and **type** of **sentences** you use. See pp. 30–31, 36–37, and 44–45.

▲ I can't tell what your conclusion is. Make sure your last paragraph wraps up your topic.

Your Turn

Now it's your turn to help the writer. Find and fix the errors in the writing. Go back to the pages in green if you need help.

1. Indent the **paragraph** that isn't indented. See pp. 58–59.

2. Find and fix the **run-on sentence**. See pp. 40–41.

3. Find and fix the two **homophone** errors. See pp. 28–29.

4. Find and fix the incorrect verb in the **past perfect tense**. See pp. 16–17.

5. Find and fix the **inconsistent verb tense**. See pp. 42–43.

6. Find and fix the **capitalization error**. See pp. 46–47.

7. Find and fix the unnecessary **quotation marks**. See pp. 56–57.

8. Find and fix the two **sentence fragments**. See pp. 34–35.

9. Find and fix the two **contraction** errors. See pp. 54–55.

USING A RUBRIC TO SCORE EXPOSITORY ESSAYS

This rubric is based on a point scale of 1 to 4. It was used to score the expository essays on pages 108–111. Use this rubric to remember what is important in expository essays.

4 A score of *4* means that the writer

- ❑ connects the writing directly to the prompt.
- ❑ almost always uses the correct forms of words.
- ❑ almost always uses capitalization and punctuation correctly.
- ❑ almost always uses clear and complete sentences and uses variety in sentences.
- ❑ uses effective words.
- ❑ creates a title that relates directly to the topic.
- ❑ clearly introduces the topic at the beginning.
- ❑ creates a strong beginning, middle, and ending.
- ❑ explains the topic with at least three main ideas, along with relevant supporting details.
- ❑ presents the ideas in an order that creates an informative essay.
- ❑ begins a new paragraph for each change of idea.

2 A score of *2* means that the writer

- ❑ connects the writing to the prompt in a general way.
- ❑ uses some incorrect forms of words.
- ❑ uses some incorrect capitalization and punctuation.
- ❑ uses little variety in sentences.
- ❑ uses some run-on or rambling sentences or sentence fragments.
- ❑ uses mostly simple words.
- ❑ creates a title that relates somewhat to the topic.
- ❑ presents the topic within the essay but uses too few main ideas or supporting details to fully explain the topic.
- ❑ creates a weak beginning, middle, or ending.
- ❑ presents the ideas in a weak or choppy order.
- ❑ may make some paragraphing errors.

3 A score of *3* means that the writer

- ❑ connects the writing to the prompt.
- ❑ usually uses the correct forms of words.
- ❑ usually uses capitalization and punctuation correctly.
- ❑ usually uses clear and complete sentences and uses some variety in sentences.
- ❑ uses some effective words.
- ❑ creates a title that relates to the essay in a general way.
- ❑ introduces the topic toward the beginning.
- ❑ creates a beginning, middle, and ending.
- ❑ explains the topic with some main ideas along with some supporting details.
- ❑ presents the ideas in an order that makes sense.
- ❑ usually begins a new paragraph for each change of idea.

1 A score of *1* means that the writer

- ❑ does not successfully connect the writing to the prompt.
- ❑ uses many incorrect forms of words.
- ❑ often uses incorrect capitalization or punctuation.
- ❑ uses almost no variety in sentences.
- ❑ uses several run-on or rambling sentences or sentence fragments.
- ❑ uses simple words.
- ❑ creates a poor title or has no title at all.
- ❑ includes the topic in the essay but uses too few main ideas or relevant supporting details to adequately explain the topic.
- ❑ creates an unclear beginning, middle, or ending.
- ❑ presents the ideas in an unclear manner.
- ❑ may make many paragraphing errors.

SCORING EXPOSITORY ESSAYS

Now it's your turn to score some expository essays. The four expository essays on pages 113 and 114 were written in response to this prompt.

> *Write an essay giving information about the ocean.*

Read each expository essay. Write a few comments about it. Then give it a score from 1 to 4. Think about what you've learned in this lesson as you match each essay with its correct score.

Model A

Score:

Under the sea

When I get older I plan to be a scientist who studies the ocean. Why? Because the ocean is fascinating.

The ocean is like a whole different world. It is full of all kinds of fish and plants and other animals. It has caves and cliffs, and even underwater mountain ranges such as the mid Atlantic ridge. In some places the water is warm. In others, there are icebergs. Some parts of the ocean are thousands of feet deep, and some are shallow. Some parts have currents that can't be predicted, and these currents are dangerous for swimmers as well as for ships.

The ocean is a fascinating place, and I want to learn more about it.

Comments: _____
_____
_____
_____
_____
_____
_____
_____

Model B

Score:

That ocean is huge and covering most of The World. It is very deep and then not very deep and theyre are way too many fish to count, plus sharks. I watch about the ocean on TV and I see them in the sub goes way down underwater and into the most darkest caves. I get afraid they will find sharks or worser things. I would like to go in that sub. Sometime. The ocean is most interesting to me.

Comments: _____
_____
_____
_____
_____
_____

Model C

Score:

The Amazing Ocean

Scientists have learned a lot about the ocean. Saltwater covers more than half the earth's surface. Ocean waters can be shallow or thousands of feet deep, and their currents can be predictable or mysterious. Ocean temperatures range from warm to icy.

Modern technology has allowed deep sea explorers to investigate the depths. From the explorers, we have learned about undersea mountain ridges and about the continental shelf. This is an underwater strip of land around each Continent. The outer edges of the shelf slope or drop off like a cliff. Below the shelf is the immense ocean floor.

What new information will scientists uncover about the ocean in years to come? Whatever it is, it will be amazing!

Comments: _____

Model D

Score:

At seas

The Ocean is big and it is all over the World. There is more than one.

There are some oceans that are called the Sea.

There are ships in the Ocean that travel around the World. They come from all over. They have been doing it since the vikings and other people.

The water in the Ocean is salty, but the fish dont mind because maybe they cant taste it, like us. The ocean has hills and mountains. It has a cliff.

Everyone knows the Ocean has sand. Some places do not. In Hawaii they have lava. That flows into the Sea.

Comments: _____

WRITING AN EXPOSITORY ESSAY

Now you get to write your own expository essay. Use the prompt below.

> *Write an essay explaining why the city or town where you live is special.*

When You Write Your Expository Essay

1. **Think about** what you want to write. Ask yourself some questions.

   - What main ideas do I want to present, and how will I order them?
   - What facts, examples, and reasons can I use to back up the ideas?
   - How will I begin my essay?
   - How will I conclude my essay?

   Use graphic organizers to gather and organize the information.

2. **Write** your first draft. Be sure your essay has a clear and effective beginning, middle, and ending.

3. **Read** your draft. Use the checklist that your teacher will give you to review your writing.

4. **Edit** your essay. Make changes until your essay gives a clear explanation of the topic.

5. **Proofread** your expository essay one last time.

6. **Write** a neat copy of your expository essay and give it to your partner.

Work with a Partner

7. **Read** your partner's expository essay.

8. **Score** your partner's expository essay from 1 to 4, using the rubric on page 112. Then complete the Partner Comments sheet that your teacher will give you. Tell what you like about the essay and what you think would make it better.

9. **Switch** papers.

10. **Think about** your partner's comments. Read your essay again. Make changes that you think will improve your expository essay.

11. **Write** a neat final copy of your expository essay.

Making Connections

- How often do you have to follow directions? Think about some directions you've heard or read recently. Were they clear, or could they have been clearer? How could you have improved them?

- In your journal, jot down a list of ordinary situations in which it may be important to give an explanation with specific examples.

- When you read your social studies or science book or when you read articles in magazines or newspapers, notice how certain text features guide you to the main ideas. Look for headings or words in bold type or large type. Also, pay attention to pictures and captions.

PERSUASIVE ESSAYS

An opinion is what you think or believe to be true about something. When you write a paper to persuade readers to agree with your opinion, you are writing a persuasive essay.

Here is a sample writing prompt for a persuasive essay.

> *Write a persuasive essay telling why people*
> *your age should or should not have the right to do something.*

Read this persuasive essay, which was written in response to the prompt. Then read the Writing Tips to learn more about persuasive essays.

Writing Tips

✳ Begin the essay by introducing the topic and your position, or opinion about it. You may also want to include an engaging fact or example to capture readers' interest.

✳ Support your position with convincing reasons that are backed up by facts and examples. Make sure your reasons are logical, and never state anything that isn't true. Devote one paragraph to each reason.

✳ Mention at least one point that those with an opposing opinion could use to challenge your argument, or position. Briefly explain why this opposing point is not as strong as your points. This part of your essay is called the "counterargument."

✳ In your essay, use carefully chosen words and precisely worded sentences. Avoid any words, comparisons, or statements that sound too personal, emotional, confusing, or weak.

✳ Use a tone that sounds confident but not rude. Remember that you want readers to agree with you, not get angry with you.

✳ Conclude your persuasive essay on a strong note. Save your strongest reason for the end.

Lights Out

Bedtime is when a person's day ends. Teens are often expected to go to bed earlier than adults do, but I think that teens should be allowed to stay up as late as adults do.

Scientific sleep studies show that the body rhythms that control sleeping and waking times change when people become teenagers. So, it's difficult for teenagers to fall asleep before midnight, even if they are tired and still need 8 to 9 hours of sleep. Some people argue that teens should not go to bed late because they won't get enough sleep if they have to get up early for school. I think this should be solved by starting school an hour later each day.

Also, teens do a lot during the day, and they need the time to do it all. Teens attend school, take part in afterschool activities or sports practices, go home, eat, relax, and then do homework.

If teens go to bed right after doing their homework, they miss out on one more important aspect of teen life, communicating with friends. This often means talking on the phone or instant messaging. Teens shouldn't have to miss out on this important part of their lives.

There's a lot packed into the day of an active teenager, and a later bedtime allows it all to happen.

USING GRAPHIC ORGANIZERS

Before you write, use **graphic organizers** to plan and arrange the reasons, facts, and examples for your persuasive essay.

The writer of the essay on page 116 might have used a Pro/Con Chart, such as the one below.

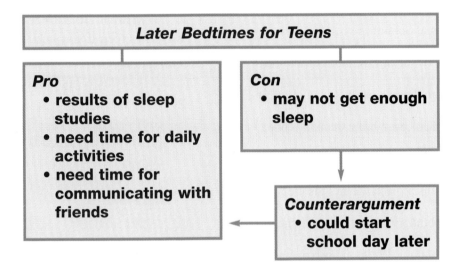

Later Bedtimes for Teens

Pro
- results of sleep studies
- need time for daily activities
- need time for communicating with friends

Con
- may not get enough sleep

Counterargument
- could start school day later

A Pro/Con Chart helps writers to organize the supporting details for their position and to identify an opposing point and counterargument.

The writer of the essay on page 116 might also have used a Details Web such as the one below. If you had been the writer, how would you have used this web? Fill in facts and examples to develop the reason related to recent sleep study results.

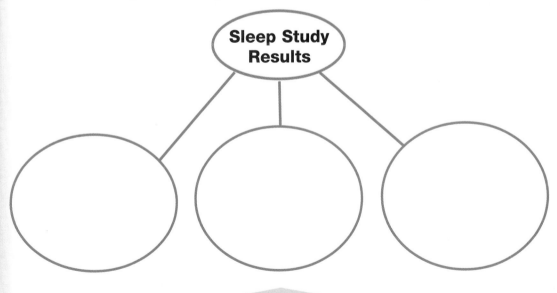

Sleep Study Results

A Details Web helps writers organize backup for the important reasons in their persuasive essays.

Score:

Read the persuasive essay below, which was written in response to the prompt on page 116. Read the comments and think about why this essay scored a 4.

Ban Cell Phones at School

The cell phone is one of the most convenient inventions of all time. Its popularity can cause problems, though. People use cell phones in cars, planes, theaters, malls, and restaurants. Kids even bring them to school, and I think that school is not the place for cell phones.

Cell phones are distracting. School is a place where kids are supposed to concentrate. When a cell phone rings in class or in the library, it disrupts everyone's train of thought. While the person answers the call, everybody sits there listening.

Cell phones are also rude. When kids at school go walking down the halls talking on cell phones, they don't mean to be impolite, but they are. It looks like theyre in their own little world and not paying attention to anyone around them. It's like they'd rather talk to people who aren't there.

Last but not least, cell phones are unnecessary. Who needs a phone at school? Some kids say they need one in case of an emergency. Yet no one is alone at school, and for important calls, there's always the pay phone. If someone from home needs to reach a student they can call the office.

In conclusion, cell phones at school are distracting, rude, and unnecessary. Since school is where students are supposed to be communicating with each other, the solution to this problem is simple. Cell phones should be left at home.

Your Turn

Now it's your turn to help the writer. Find and fix the errors in the writing. Go back to the pages in green if you need help.

1. Find and fix the **contraction** error. See pp. 54–55.
2. Find and fix the missing **comma** after an **introductory dependent clause**. See pp. 52–53.

TEACHER COMMENTS

4

▲ The first paragraph gets my attention and states your opinion.

▲ You have arranged your points in a logical order, with the most important point at the end. This builds up readers' agreement with your position.

▲ You have chosen your words carefully and have used a variety of sentences.

▲ I'm glad you included the opposing point about emergencies, along with the counterargument. Your argument is stronger as a result.

▲ Your concluding paragraph ties up the argument nicely and restates your main opinion. Well done!

PARTNER COMMENTS

2   3

This was really good. You actually changed my opinion about cell phones in school.

Read the persuasive essay and the comments that follow. Think about why this essay scored a 3.

Hang It Up!

Cell phones at school is getting to be a problem. Kids have started carrying them all over, even to class. This should not be allowed.

One reason for the problem is that you never know when the cell phones are going to ring. If one rings in class, it disturbs everybody. That can be annoying for the teacher and for the students. What if someone is in the middle of an oral report? That's the worse time of all to be interrupted.

Kids talking on cell phones are also not being very polite to their friends. How can you have a conversation with someone who is always on the phone? Its obviously rude. I have one friend who hardly knows me anymore because his phone always buzzes before I'm finished with what I'm saying! I think everybody should have better manners.

I know that some kids say that they want a cell phone in case of an emergency or something. I don't see what they are so worried about.

Don't get me wrong; I'm not against cell phones on principal. I own one myself, but I would never bring it to school. School is a place where cell phones really do not belong. They should not be aloud.

Your Turn

Now it's your turn to help the writer. Find and fix the errors in the writing. Go back to the pages in green if you need help.

1. Find and fix the error in **subject-verb agreement**. See pp. 18–19.
2. Find and fix the incorrect **adjective** showing **comparison**. See pp. 22–23.
3. Find and fix the **contraction** that is missing an **apostrophe**. See pp. 54–55.
4. Find and fix the **unnecessary phrase**. See pp. 42–43.
5. Find and fix the two **homophone** errors. See pp. 28–29.

TEACHER COMMENTS

▲ You have clearly presented your opinion in the first paragraph. Thank you.

▲ You have presented your reasons in a logical order and have backed up each reason with examples. Your argument would sound more authoritative, however, if you used more facts and relied less on your own feelings and personal opinions.

▲ You do present an opposing opinion, but you should counter it with a stronger argument of your own.

▲ You have a clear concluding paragraph, but it would be stronger if it was less personal.

PARTNER COMMENTS

Your position was pretty clear, but you didn't explain what was wrong with the opposing argument. That was the only part I didn't understand.

Score:

Read the persuasive essay and the comments that follow. Think about why this essay scored a 2.

1

The New Thing

There is a new thing at school. Kids are bringing cell phones to class, and this causes problems. Well I dont have anything against cell phones but I think they shouldnt be in class.

Maybe I do not like them because kids with them looks stupid. I saw a girl talking the other day and she was sitting outside at lunch time, and she is all alone except for a headset. Everyone does that now.

Kids say they have a right to bring them.

Cell phones in school is ringing in class all the time. How can we think? They should be against the rules. Thats the only way to fix the problem.

2

Your Turn

Now it's your turn to help the writer. Find and fix the errors in the writing. Go back to the pages in green if you need help.

1. Indent the **paragraph** that isn't indented. See pp. 58–59.
2. Find and fix the missing **comma** after an **introductory word**. See pp. 52–53.
3. Find and fix the three **contraction** errors. See pp. 54–55.
4. Find and fix the **compound sentence** that is missing a **comma**. See pp. 30–31.
5. Find and fix the two errors in **subject-verb agreement**. See pp. 18–19.
6. Find and fix the **rambling sentence**. See pp. 40–41.
7. Find and fix the **inconsistent verb tense**. See pp. 42–43.

PARTNER COMMENTS

I could tell that you were trying to make a point against allowing cell phones at school, but your argument was too hard to follow.

TEACHER COMMENTS

4

▲ Your title should relate directly to your opinion.

▲ I'd like to see you use more variety with **words** and **sentences**. In your first paragraph, the word *class* appears three times. See pp. 4–5, 22–27, and 44–45 for help.

▲ Try to avoid using words like *stupid*. It is impolite and could offend readers.

▲ You need to clarify the reasons for your opinion and back up each reason with facts and examples.

▲ Be careful not to introduce irrelevant details or personal issues. Most of the middle of your essay is devoted to a personal perspective.

▲ You mention an opposing argument, but you don't explain or refute it. Take your time. Tell why kids feel they have a right to bring cell phones to school.

▲ You conclude your essay with a strong personal opinion. Can you add a fact?

Read the persuasive essay and the comments that follow.
Think about why this essay scored a 1.

Ring, Not!

Some kids think its so cool to have a cell phone in their pocket everywhere they go. I think phones in a school is not cool. They cause accidents and to look silly. Just fed up! People should hang up and drive. Like that bumper sticker on all the cars say. Phones in school make me real upset. My parents theirselves don't have one most of my friends parents don't have one. Kids like I shouldnt have cell phones.

PARTNER COMMENTS

You didn't follow the prompt. You were supposed to write a persuasive essay, giving an opinion and backing it up. It's clear that you're not crazy about cell phones, though.

2

TEACHER COMMENTS

3

▲ Your title is clever, and it certainly gets my attention.

▲ You didn't follow the prompt very well. You were supposed to write a persuasive essay, presenting an opinion and supporting it with reasons, facts, and examples. This isn't long enough to be an essay. Although you present many personal opinions and feelings, you don't present a central opinion, creating a strong argument so that readers will agree with you.

▲ You definitely have some strong feelings about cell phones. You should take your time to focus your ideas. Think about sorting out your reasons and creating more separate **paragraphs** to organize them. *See pp. 58–59 for help.*

▲ Try to use more variety in the **structure** and **type of sentences** you use. *See pp. 30–31, 36–37, and 44–45.*

▲ Try beginning some sentences with **modifiers**. *See pp. 32–33.*

Your Turn

Now it's your turn to help the writer. Find and fix the errors in the writing. Go back to the pages in green if you need help.

1. Find and fix the two **contractions** that are missing an **apostrophe**. See pp. 54–55.

2. Find and fix the two errors in **subject-verb agreement**. See pp. 18–19.

3. Find and fix the sentence that lacks **parallel structure**. See pp. 42–43.

4. Find and fix the two **sentence fragments**. See pp. 34–35.

5. Find and fix the **adjective** that should be an **adverb**. See pp. 26–27.

6. Find and fix the **run-on sentence**. See pp. 40–41.

7. Find and fix the incorrect **reflexive pronoun**. See pp. 14–15.

8. Find and fix the incorrect **possessive noun**. See pp. 8–9.

9. Find and fix the incorrect **object pronoun**. See pp. 10–11.

4

USING A RUBRIC TO SCORE PERSUASIVE ESSAYS

This rubric is based on a point scale of 1 to 4. It was used to score the persuasive essays on pages 118–121. Use the rubric to remember what is important in persuasive essays.

4 A score of 4 means that the writer

- ❑ connects the writing directly to the prompt.
- ❑ almost always uses the correct forms of words.
- ❑ almost always uses capitalization and punctuation correctly.
- ❑ almost always uses clear and complete sentences and uses variety in sentences.
- ❑ uses effective words.
- ❑ creates a title that relates to the opinion.
- ❑ presents a clear beginning, middle, and ending.
- ❑ clearly introduces the topic and opinion in the beginning.
- ❑ backs up the opinion with strong reasons, facts, and examples.
- ❑ presents the ideas in an order that strengthens the opinion.
- ❑ clearly anticipates and counters at least one objection.
- ❑ begins a new paragraph for each change of idea.

2 A score of 2 means that the writer

- ❑ connects the writing to the prompt in a general way.
- ❑ uses some incorrect forms of words.
- ❑ uses some incorrect capitalization or punctuation.
- ❑ uses little variety in sentences.
- ❑ uses some run-on or rambling sentences or sentence fragments.
- ❑ uses mostly simple words.
- ❑ creates a title.
- ❑ presents a weak beginning, middle, or ending.
- ❑ presents a weak or confusing opinion.
- ❑ may provide too few reasons, facts, or examples to support the opinion.
- ❑ presents the ideas in an unclear order.
- ❑ weakly anticipates or addresses a possible objection.
- ❑ may make some paragraphing errors.

3 A score of 3 means that the writer

- ❑ connects the writing to the prompt.
- ❑ usually uses the correct forms of words.
- ❑ usually uses capitalization and punctuation correctly.
- ❑ usually uses clear and complete sentences and uses variety in sentences.
- ❑ uses some effective words.
- ❑ creates a title that generally relates to the opinion.
- ❑ presents a beginning, middle, and ending.
- ❑ introduces the topic and opinion in the beginning.
- ❑ backs up the opinion with some strong reasons, facts, and examples.
- ❑ presents the ideas in an order that makes sense.
- ❑ anticipates and counters at least one objection.
- ❑ usually begins a new paragraph for each change of idea.

1 A score of 1 means that the writer

- ❑ does not successfully connect the writing to the prompt.
- ❑ uses many incorrect forms of words.
- ❑ often uses incorrect capitalization or punctuation.
- ❑ uses almost no variety in sentences.
- ❑ uses many run-on or rambling sentences or sentence fragments.
- ❑ uses simple or inappropriate words.
- ❑ usually creates a poor title or no title at all.
- ❑ presents an unclear beginning, middle, or ending.
- ❑ may not state the opinion or does not provide enough reasons, facts, or examples to back up the opinion.
- ❑ may include unimportant details.
- ❑ presents the ideas in a confusing order.
- ❑ fails to anticipate or address a possible objection.
- ❑ may make many paragraphing errors.

SCORING PERSUASIVE ESSAYS

Now it's your turn to score some persuasive essays. The four essays on pages 123 and 124 were written in response to this prompt.

> *Write an essay giving your opinion about the best color for a bedroom ceiling.*

Read each persuasive essay. Write a few comments about it. Then give it a score from 1 to 4. Think about what you've learned in this lesson as you match each persuasive essay with its correct score.

Model A

Score: ▽

Not To Blue

If your asking me what color is best for my bedroom ceiling I will say pale blue. I know someone who painted there hole room Navy but that is to dark. It could make you think it was night, when its not.

It could be pink too, my sisters' was, she loved it.

My parents is only white. Boring!

The best color for the ceiling is pale blue. No matter what you say. It is light and cool and relaxed.

Comments: _____

_____

_____

_____

_____

_____

_____

_____

Model B

Score: ▽

Flying

I dont always admit this, ever since I was little, I dream of flying up and away. I closed my eyes and before I know it the ceiling was turning into a dome and I was flying around up there and out into the sky where I was a hero against all them bad guys below. Thats the reason my room and ceiling is blue. I like light blue for my room. Some people say "give me desert colors, but I couldn't never sleep good under a red or orange or yellow sky. No way. Give me Blue!

Comments: _____

_____

_____

_____

_____

_____

Model C

Score: ▽

Light and Breezy

One of the most important things people can do is choose a good color for their bedroom ceiling.

In my opinion, light blue is the best color, for two main reasons. First, light blue makes a person think of coolness. Things that are light blue include water and ice. Second, light blue makes a person think of the sky, and the sky is made of air. Thinking of air makes you imagine the feeling of lightness. Those who decide to have a red ceiling may wonder why they can't get to sleep. Two things they are missing are the feelings of coolness and lightness!

They need a light blue ceiling!

Comments: _____

_____

_____

_____

_____

_____

_____

Model D

Score: ▽

Sky Blue

Your bedroom is mostly where you sleep, but sometimes you're awake and looking up at your ceiling. That's when you realize that the best color for a ceiling is sky blue.

The main reason to have a sky blue ceiling is that it is like looking into the sky. If people are gazing at their bedroom ceiling, they will naturally feel relaxed if the ceiling looks like an airy space. By contrast, they might feel seasick if the ceiling looked like a green ocean.

Another reason for having a sky blue bedroom ceiling is that it looks cool. Most people sleep better in a room that isn't too warm. Just the sight of a light blue ceiling makes you feel cooler than a bright pink ceiling on a hot day would.

Sky blue is the best bedroom ceiling color. It's so peaceful and cool, you drift to sleep as if you're floating on a cloud.

Comments: _____

_____

_____

_____

_____

_____

_____

WRITING A PERSUASIVE ESSAY

Now you get to write your own persuasive essay. Use the prompt below.

> *Write a persuasive essay about something that*
> *you think should be changed in the world.*

When You Write Your Persuasive Essay

1. **Think about** what you want to write. Ask yourself some questions.

   • What is my opinion?
   • What examples or facts can I use to support my reasons
     for the opinion?
   • In what order should I present my reasons?
   • How might someone oppose my opinion? How could I argue
     against the opposition?

   Use graphic organizers to arrange your reasons, facts, and examples.

2. **Write** your first draft. Keep in mind that you want to persuade
   readers to agree with your opinion.

3. **Read** your draft. Use the checklist that your teacher will give you
   to review your writing.

4. **Edit** your essay. Make changes until your essay presents a strong
   and logical argument.

5. **Proofread** your persuasive essay one last time.

6. **Write** a neat copy of your persuasive essay and give it
   to your partner.

Work with a Partner

7. **Read** your partner's persuasive essay.

8. **Score** your partner's persuasive essay from 1 to 4, using the rubric
   on page 122. Then complete the Partner Comments sheet that your
   teacher will give you. Tell what you like about the essay and what
   you think would make it better.

9. **Switch** papers.

10. **Think about** your partner's comments. Read your essay again.
    Make changes that you think will improve your persuasive essay.

11. **Write** a neat final copy of your persuasive essay.

Making Connections

♦ Opinions appear in many
  kinds of writing. Look for
  them in ads, book and
  movie reviews, letters to
  the editor in newspapers
  and magazines, and the
  voices of characters
  in stories, plays, and
  movies. Ask yourself
  which opinions you
  agree with, and why.

♦ In your journal, make
  notes on your reactions
  to news and talk shows
  on TV. What do you think
  of the opinions people
  express? Are they
  persuasive? Why or
  why not?

♦ As you listen to friends
  and other people talk,
  think about the different
  ways they express their
  opinions. Which ways are
  more likely to convince
  you that they could
  be right?

♦ Use what you learn
  about these persuasive
  presentations to
  strengthen your own
  persuasive writing.

Summarizing is one way to show that you understand what you have read. A summary is a brief restatement of the most important points of a longer piece of writing. In a summary of fiction, you briefly present the characters and plot events. In a summary of nonfiction, you briefly state the main ideas and essential details in your own words.

Here is a sample writing prompt for a summary of a nonfiction article.

> *Read the article "Libraries, Then and Now" on page 127.*
> *Then write a summary of it.*

Read the article on page 127 and read the summary below, which was written in response to the prompt. Then read the Writing Tips to learn more about summaries.

Writing Tips

❖ At the beginning of the summary, mention the topic of the article. Then paraphrase, or restate in your own words, the article's main ideas and any essential supporting details.

❖ Headings printed in bold type in the article can help you identify main ideas.

❖ Your summary should be only one paragraph long, so be concise.

❖ Arrange the ideas in the order in which the author presented them in the main article.

❖ Use your own words whenever possible. It's all right to use some key words, facts, or details, but avoid copying long passages of text from the article.

❖ Keep the summary clear and simple. Avoid colorful language unless it relates to the article.

❖ Never add to a summary any ideas or opinions that are not contained in the original work. Stick strictly to what the author wrote.

When people first began making copies of written works, they needed places to put them. The first libraries were in ancient Mesopotamia. They contained clay tablets on which records, stories, and letters were marked. Ancient Egyptian libraries preserved writings on scrolls of papyrus. During the Middle Ages, writings on parchment filled monastery libraries in Europe. Library books on paper became common only after the invention of the printing press in the 1400s. Today, libraries around the world contain many types of works, including written texts, audiovisual materials, and other resources.

Here is the article from which the summary on page 126 was written.

LIBRARIES, THEN AND NOW

In early periods of history, people around the world had no books. Instead, they painted and carved symbols and images on stone, wood, and other materials. Later, once people began making multiple copies of written works, the works began to accumulate. Then readers and scholars needed places to put them.

Ancient Libraries

The first known libraries, established 5,000 years ago in ancient Mesopotamia, contained collections of clay tablets. These tablets preserved records, stories, and personal letters. When the clay was wet, the tablets were marked with a tool, such as a stick or reed. Then the tablets were dried in the sun.

Libraries in ancient Egypt contained information written on papyrus scrolls, which were made from papyrus reeds taken from the Nile River. The papyrus was processed by cutting the stems into strips and pressing the strips into sheets. Then the sheets were joined together to form scrolls.

Libraries in the Middle Ages

By the Middle Ages, some libraries housed works written on parchment, a paperlike material made from animal skins. In Constantinople, a library preserved parchment copies of Roman laws. European libraries flourished in monasteries, where monks copied religious writings onto parchment.

When paper was invented in China in A.D. 105, the first handwritten paper books were made and stored in Asian libraries. However, paper was not introduced to Europe until centuries later. Not until the printing press was invented in the 1400s did printed paper books become common in the libraries of Europe.

Modern Libraries

Modern libraries in towns, cities, schools, colleges, and universities around the world contain many kinds of works, created from different materials and stored in various forms. Written texts make up most of a library's collections—in books, magazines, newspapers, pamphlets, manuscripts, and electronic files. The largest libraries also contain audiovisual resources, such as records, tapes, films, maps, photographs, and paintings, as well as collections for people with special needs.

Libraries, ancient to modern, serve as repositories for the records of history.

Before you write, use graphic organizers to gather and organize the most important ideas for your summary.

The writer of the summary on page 126 might have used a Topic/Main Ideas Chart such as the one below.

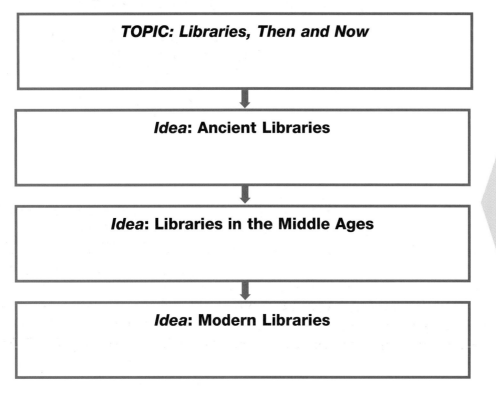

TOPIC: Libraries, Then and Now

Idea: Ancient Libraries

Idea: Libraries in the Middle Ages

Idea: Modern Libraries

A Topic/Main Ideas Chart helps writers identify the most important ideas in an article, from which a summary can be written.

The writer of the summary on page 126 might also have used a Main Idea/Details Web. If you had been the writer, how would you have used the web below? Fill in details for the main idea given in the center oval of the web.

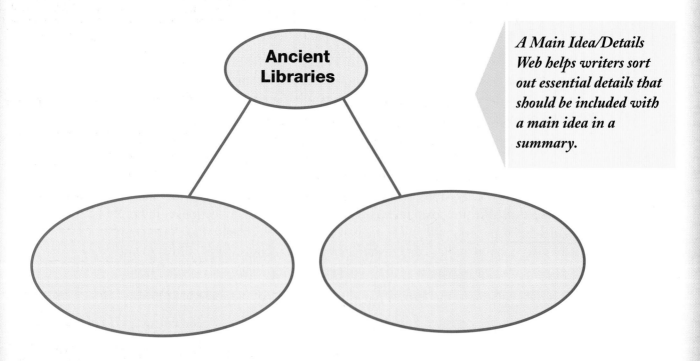

Ancient Libraries

A Main Idea/Details Web helps writers sort out essential details that should be included with a main idea in a summary.

TAKING A LOOK AT SUMMARIES

Read the summary below. It was written in response to the prompt on page 126. Read the comments and think about why this summary scored a 4.

The earliest libraries that we know about developed in ancient Mesopotamia 5,000 years ago. They contained clay tablets covered with markings. Ancient Egyptian libraries contained writings on scrolls made of papyrus. Later, during the Middle ages, libraries in Constantinople and Europe collected writings on parchment. The first paper books were made in China, and stored in Asian libraries. Today, modern libraries around the world contain collections that have been created from various materials and are stored in different forms.

2

PARTNER COMMENTS

3

I liked your summary because it covered all the main ideas from the article. Reading this summary gave me a clear idea of what the article was about.

Your Turn

Now it's your turn to help the writer. Find and fix the errors in the writing. Go back to the pages in green if you need help.

1. Find and fix the **capitalization** error. See pp. 50–51.
2. Find and fix the incorrect **comma** in a **simple sentence** with a **compound predicate.** See pp. 30–31.

TEACHER COMMENTS

4

▲ You clearly followed the writing prompt.

▲ You've done a nice job of paraphrasing the most important ideas and details in the article.

▲ Other than key terms such as *scrolls* and *papyrus*, you have used your own words and have chosen effective ones.

▲ By using transitional words, such as *later* and *today*, you've clarified the order of the ideas. Good!

▲ You have presented the ideas in the order in which they are presented in the article.

▲ You have focused on the content of the article and have not introduced any new ideas or opinions. Good job!

Score:

3

Read the summary and the comments that follow. Think about why this summary scored a 3.

1

In the beginning, people didn't have libraries because they didn't have books. These people wrote on clay tablets, and on papyrus scrolls. By the Middle Ages, people wrote on sheets of dried animal skin. Called parchment. Books weren't printed on paper yet because there was no paper, and there were no printing presses. Only libraries in Europe got printed books after the printing press had been invented. Modern Libraries have almost every kind of work there was.

2

Your Turn

Now it's your turn to help the writer. Find and fix the errors in the writing. Go back to the pages in green if you need help.

1. Find and fix the **comma** used incorrectly in a **simple sentence**. See pp. 30–31.
2. Find and fix the **sentence fragment**. See pp. 34–35.
3. Find and fix the **misplaced modifier** (one word). See pp. 32–33.
4. Find and fix the **capitalization** error. See pp. 48–49.
5. Find and fix the **inconsistent verb tense**. See pp. 42–43.

PARTNER COMMENTS

You covered some of the article's main points, but you left out some important ones, too. I could tell what the article was generally about, though.

3

TEACHER COMMENTS

4

 You've followed the prompt and have introduced the topic early on. Good!

 You've included some of the article's most important ideas. You might have presented some ideas more clearly, however. What does it mean that modern libraries have "almost every kind of work"?

 You did a good job of presenting ideas in the same order as they appear in the article.

 You could use some **transitional words** to connect the ideas more clearly. See pp. 60–61 for help.

**Read the summary and the comments that follow.
Think about why this summary scored a 2.**

1

The first libraries had clay tablets. The second oldest collections were in Egypts libraries. They had papyrus scrolls, some other libraries were in Asia. In China, they made books by hand from paper. That was when they invents paper. The next oldest libraries were in the middle Ages. They had parchment. Its' made from animal skin. They invented the printing press in the 1400s and now libraries are all over the World, and they have books and things for special "people".

Your Turn

Now it's your turn to help the writer. Find and fix the errors in the writing. Go back to the pages in green if you need help.

1. Find and fix the incorrect **possessive noun**. See pp. 8–9.

2. Find and fix the **run-on sentence**. See pp. 40–41.

3. Find and fix the **inconsistent verb tense**. See pp. 42–43.

4. Find and fix the two **capitalization** errors. See pp. 48–51.

5. Find and fix the **contraction** error. See pp. 54–55.

6. Find and fix the **rambling sentence**. See pp. 40–41.

7. Find and fix the pair of **quotation marks** used incorrectly. See pp. 56–57.

2

PARTNER COMMENTS

3

I could tell that the article had something to do with libraries, but the topic was unclear. The order of your ideas was confusing too.

TEACHER COMMENTS

4

▲ I'm glad to see you have used words that reflect some of the article's main ideas and key details.

▲ Check to make sure your statements are complete and accurate.

▲ When you mention the invention of the printing press, the sequence of events is out of order. Be careful to follow the author's order exactly.

▲ Try using some **nouns** instead of relying on the pronoun *they*. See pp. 4–5 for help.

Score:

1

Read the summary and the comments that follow.
Think about why this summary scored a 1.

1

In early days, people wrote on wet clay tables. That they dried in the sun. Then there was Papyrus. It was taken from the Nile river. Then they invented paper and the printing press and then they started to make books. Long ago they wrote simple. They wrote by hand. Now most of us is using computers. Theres library stuff on the Internet. There are no video games. It is to boring for me. I say "Give me games!"

PARTNER COMMENTS

2

I couldn't tell from your summary what the article was about. The different periods of time that you mentioned weren't clear. You made lots of errors.

3

TEACHER COMMENTS

▲ Make sure you use the correct forms of words. Don't use *tables* if the article says *tablets*. Remember, you can quote key words.

▲ You haven't summarized all the important ideas from the article. Use a graphic organizer to make sure you cover them all.

4

▲ Your summary doesn't paraphrase ideas in the order in which the author presented them. Try using the article's headings to identify the main ideas and their order.

▲ Remember not to state any opinions or information other than what is in the article. When you say "It is boring," you're expressing your opinion.

▲ Use different **types** of **sentences** and **different beginnings**. See pp. 30–31 and 44–45 for help.

Your Turn

Now it's your turn to help the writer. Find and fix the errors in the writing. Go back to the pages in green if you need help.

1. Indent the **paragraph**. See pp. 58–59.

2. Find and fix the **sentence fragment**. See pp. 34–35.

3. Find and fix the two **capitalization** errors. See pp. 48–51.

4. Find and fix the **rambling sentence**. See pp. 40–41.

5. Find and fix the **adjective** that should be an **adverb**. See pp. 26–27.

6. Find and fix the error in **subject-verb agreement**. See pp. 20–21.

7. Find and fix the **contraction** error. See pp. 54–55.

8. Find and fix the incorrect **homophone**. See pp. 28–29.

9. Find and fix the **comma** missing from a **direct quote**. See pp. 56–57.

USING A RUBRIC TO SCORE SUMMARIES

This rubric is based on a point scale of 1 to 4. It was used to score the summaries on pages 129–132. Use the rubric to remember what is important in summaries.

④ A score of *4* means that the writer

- ❏ connects the writing directly to the prompt.
- ❏ almost always uses the correct forms of words.
- ❏ almost always uses capitalization and punctuation correctly.
- ❏ almost always uses clear and complete sentences and appropriate variety in sentences.
- ❏ uses effective words.
- ❏ presents the topic at the beginning of the summary.
- ❏ includes only the most important ideas and necessary supporting details from the article.
- ❏ does not add new information or opinions.
- ❏ uses his or her own words effectively, with necessary key terms from the article.
- ❏ presents ideas in the same order as they are presented in the article.

② A score of *2* means that the writer

- ❏ connects the writing to the prompt in a general way.
- ❏ uses some incorrect forms of words.
- ❏ uses some incorrect capitalization or punctuation.
- ❏ uses little variety in sentences.
- ❏ uses some run-on or rambling sentences or sentence fragments.
- ❏ uses mostly simple words.
- ❏ may not clearly present the topic.
- ❏ includes some important ideas from the main article but may also include unimportant ideas or details.
- ❏ may add new information or opinions or may copy text from the passage.
- ❏ uses his or her own words, but they may not reflect the ideas of the article.
- ❏ presents some ideas that do not follow the order of the ideas in the article.

③ A score of *3* means that the writer

- ❏ connects the writing directly to the prompt.
- ❏ usually uses the correct forms of words.
- ❏ usually uses capitalization and punctuation correctly.
- ❏ usually uses clear and complete sentences and some variety in sentences.
- ❏ uses some effective words.
- ❏ presents the topic toward the beginning of the summary.
- ❏ includes many important ideas and necessary details from the main article.
- ❏ may add new information or opinions.
- ❏ uses his or her own words, with some key terms from the article.
- ❏ presents all or most ideas in the same order as they are presented in the article.

① A score of *1* means that the writer

- ❏ does not successfully connect the writing to the prompt.
- ❏ uses many incorrect forms of words.
- ❏ often uses incorrect capitalization or punctuation.
- ❏ uses almost no variety in sentences.
- ❏ uses many run-on or rambling sentences or sentence fragments.
- ❏ uses simple or inappropriate words.
- ❏ may not state the topic.
- ❏ includes only a few important ideas from the article.
- ❏ often adds new information or opinions and may copy text from the article.
- ❏ presents many ideas that do not follow the order of the ideas in the article.

SCORING SUMMARIES

Now it's your turn to score some summaries. The four summaries on this page were written in response to this prompt.

> *Read the article "California Condor" on page 135. Then write a summary of it.*

Read each summary. Write a few comments about it. Then give it a score from 1 to 4. Think about what you've learned in this lesson as you match each summary with its correct score.

Model A

Score:

The California condor, the largest land bird in North America, is a type of vulture. It needs a large area in which to search for carrion. California condors raise few young and are vulnerable to poisoning, pesticides, and habitat destruction due to construction. That's why they have become an endangered species. Scientists have been breeding condors in captivity and hope to be releasing them by 2010.

Comments: _____

_____

_____

_____

Model C

Score:

California condors are the biggest birds on earth. They fly high and fast and eat carrion. The California condor is practically extinct, though, because it is threatened by bullets, pesticides, and buildings that are in its way. In 1985 biologists had to take the last wild birds away to breed them so they wouldn't die out. They don't know yet if their plan worked, but hopefully it did.

Comments: _____

_____

_____

_____

Model B

Score:

California condors can fly almost 3 miles high and go through the air as fast as a car, awesome. They eat dead animals which is gross, but hey thats because there vultures. There an endangered species which is no accident. The reason is because of the dangers of the wild. Their was almost no more condors left when people came and took them away and their trying to rescue them.

Comments: _____

_____

_____

_____

Model D

Score:

Condor, the name of the biggest bird in california. Almost as big as a plane I think! That bird flyes high as a mountain. It wont live long if people don't save them and so some people tried and they don't know yet. Vultures eat dead animals called carrion so they get poisoned. I would warn them for sure.

Comments: _____

_____

_____

_____

Here is the article from which the summaries on page 134 were written.

CALIFORNIA CONDOR

The largest land bird in North America is a type of vulture called the California condor. An adult weighs about 22 pounds and has a wingspan of over 9 feet.

Habitat

Condors prefer a warm, dry climate and a large expanse of open grasslands, oak woodlands, or mountain foothills. They do not build nests but roost high in trees, caves, or cliffside outcroppings.

Flight and Food

From their roosts, condors take flight on warm air currents called thermals. They soar for hours, their sharp eyes searching for food on land below. Gliding at altitudes as high as 15,000 feet and at speeds greater than 55 miles per hour, they can travel 140 miles or more a day.

Like most vultures, condors do not kill to eat. They devour carrion, the flesh of dead animals. They prefer the carrion of large animals such as sheep, deer, and cattle. When they find a carcass, they gorge on it and may not need to eat again for several days.

Breeding and Rearing

Adult condor pairs form long-term bonds, although they do not breed every year. The female lays only 1 egg, which is 4 inches long. The male helps to incubate the egg, or keep it warm. It takes two months for the white, downy chick to hatch. The chick remains dependent on its parents for a year or more. If the chick survives the dangers of life in the wild, it could live 20 to 40 years.

Decline and Recovery

Since 1967, the California condor has been listed as an endangered species. Lead bullets in the flesh of carrion that condors ate had poisoned them, pesticides such as DDT had weakened the shells of their eggs, and housing developments had reduced their habitat. In 1977, 45 birds were counted in the wild. By 1985, only 9 were left.

Biologists took the last wild birds to facilities where they could be protected and bred in captivity. Their goal was to breed and eventually release 15 breeding pairs of California condors into carefully selected wild habitats by 2010. They hope that the birds' population will grow back to at least 150. The rescue plan appears to be working, but it is too early to be sure.

WRITING A SUMMARY

Now you get to write your own summary. Use the prompt below.

> *Read the article "Dorothea Lange" on page 137.*
> *Then write a summary of it.*

Making Connections

- Tonight write a summary of today's events in your journal.

- Write a summary of a news report that you hear on the radio, watch on TV, or read in the paper. This will give you practice getting the most out of the information that comes your way.

- The next time you watch a popular movie, write a summary of it. Then compare your summary to one you find in a magazine or newspaper.

- If you are asked in class to write a summary of a chapter or an article, remember to use the headings and any words in bold or italic type as guides to the most important ideas.

When You Write Your Summary

1. **Think about** what you want to write. Ask yourself some questions.
   - What is the topic of the main article?
   - How can I use the section headings to organize the main ideas for the summary?
   - What are the main ideas of the article?
   - Are there any important terms I need to mention?

   Use graphic organizers to gather and sort the information.

2. **Write** your first draft. Remember that a summary should be brief. Try to write one or two sentences for each main idea.

3. **Read** your draft. Use the checklist that your teacher will give you to review your writing.

4. **Edit** your summary. Make sure the important ideas are concisely stated, in the same order as they appear in the main article.

5. **Proofread** your summary one last time.

6. **Write** a neat copy of your summary and give it to your partner.

Work with a Partner

7. **Read** your partner's summary.

8. **Score** your partner's summary from 1 to 4, using the rubric on page 133. Then complete the Partner Comments sheet that your teacher will give you. Tell what you like about the summary and what you think would make it better.

9. **Switch** papers.

10. **Think about** your partner's comments. Read your summary again. Make any changes that you think will improve your summary.

11. **Write** a neat final copy of your summary.

DOROTHEA LANGE

When Dorothea Lange was born in 1895, in Hoboken, New Jersey, she had no idea that she would grow up to be famous. However, today she is known as an artist who showed the world how Americans lived during the Great Depression and World War II.

Finding Her Direction

When she was seven, Lange suffered from polio, a terrible but common disease that permanently crippled her legs and made her walk with a limp. When Dorothea was twelve, her father left the family, and her mother went to work as a librarian. On her way to school in New York City, Dorothea found herself noticing many poor and homeless people.

By the age of 18, Lange had decided that she wanted to become a photographer. She wanted to record the human life that she saw. Taking classes and working as an apprentice, she began learning how to take pictures and develop them in a darkroom.

Discovering Her Subjects

During the Great Depression of the 1930s, Lange photographed poor farming families whose crops had failed from drought. Many of these people had migrated west to earn a living laboring in the fields of California. Among Lange's most famous pictures was a portrait of a 32-year-old widow from Oklahoma, shown to the right. The woman and her 7 children had been surviving on frozen vegetables from the fields they worked and from birds that the children caught. This portrait, called "Migrant Mother," helped to call attention to the hardships suffered by migrant workers in those days.

During World War II, Lange took photographs of life in western internment camps where the U.S. War Relocation Authority forced 110,000 Japanese Americans to live from 1942 to 1946. Again, Lange's photographs communicated a powerful message. It was that the government should free everyone in the camps.

Using Her Tool

Although Dorothea Lange did not think of her pictures as art, other people did. When her pictures appeared in newspapers and magazines, she intended them to tell a true, if painful, story. To Lange, a camera was a window through which a photographer revealed the world to others. She once said, "One should really use the camera as though tomorrow you'd be stricken blind."

A test prompt for expository writing assumes that you will use facts, examples, and reasons that you already know. In class, however, you are sometimes asked to write **research reports** about real people, places, or things. For research reports, you need to add to what you already know with information from other sources.

TOPIC

When you are assigned a research report, you might be given a specific topic, or you might be given a general topic that you will need to narrow down. Here's an example of a prompt for a general topic: *Describe an environmental problem and propose ways to solve it.*

You can narrow the topic by asking yourself some questions. What environmental problem do I want to investigate? Air pollution? Water pollution? Soil pollution?

If you choose to investigate soil pollution, use what you already know and pose further questions to narrow your focus. Will you write about soil pollution from chemicals? Oil spills? Plastic bags?

If you choose to report on soil pollution resulting from discarded plastic bags, you will need to gather information about the problem and the possible solutions.

SOURCES

Once you have sufficiently narrowed your topic, it's then time to gather information. **Sources** you might use at home or in the library include nonfiction books, encyclopedias, researched magazine articles, maps or atlases, and the Internet.

NOTES

Once you've found your sources, take **notes** to help yourself remember the most important information that you find. You might list the notes in a notebook or write them on index cards

As you take notes, begin making a **bibliography**, a list of your sources. For each source, list the title, author, date of publication, publisher, city, volume number, and page(s). For each website, list the Internet address. You may be asked to include a bibliography with your report.

ORGANIZATION

One way to begin to arrange the information for your report is to use a **graphic organizer** that is appropriate for the organizational format of the report. Since this report is organized around a problem/solutions format, you could use a Problem/Solutions Diagram. The writer of the report on page 140 might have begun with a diagram such as this.

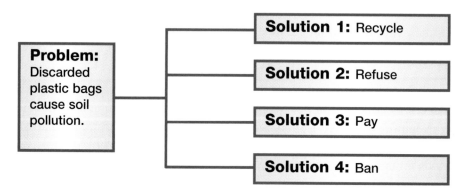

Problem: Discarded plastic bags cause soil pollution.

Solution 1: Recycle

Solution 2: Refuse

Solution 3: Pay

Solution 4: Ban

Once you have completed a graphic organizer, you can add details to create an **outline**, from which you can write the body of your report. For an outline, begin by stating the **report topic** at the top. For the outline for this report, you would list each of the 4 solutions. Then you would fill in details about the solutions. The details would be the pros (advantages) and the cons (disadvantages) of each solution. Use the report on page 140 to fill in the outline below. The main ideas have been filled in, and one example is provided.

Solutions to Soil Pollution from Plastic Bags

I. **Solution 1: Recycle**
  A. 1990, through U.S. supermarkets
  B. _____
  C. _____

II. **Solution 2: Refuse**
  A. _____
  B. _____
    1. _____
    2. _____

III. **Solution 3: Pay**
  A. _____
  B. _____
    1. _____
    2. _____

IV. **Solution 4: Ban**
  A. _____
    1. _____
    2. _____
  B. _____

In addition to ideas and details from the outline, your report should include an **opening paragraph**, or *introduction*, and a **closing paragraph**, or *conclusion*. Your final report should follow this format:

Beginning A strong title and an opening paragraph that introduces the topic and grabs readers' attention with a lead.

Middle Main ideas and supporting details that build the body of the report, using information listed on the outline. Each main idea should have its own paragraph.

Ending A closing paragraph that sums up the ideas in the report, restates the topic in different words, or gives an overview of the report. It should provide a sense of closure for readers.

Here is a research report that describes the problem and some solutions to the issue of soil pollution from discarded plastic bags. The writer used the graphic organizer on page 138 to plan the content of the report and the outline on page 139 to write a draft. The writer then edited and proofread the report. The final report scored a 4. It will be published in a local newspaper.

What to Do About Plastic Bags

Beginning

What would life be like without plastic bags? Although this common convenience has only been around since the 1960s, many people in industrialized countries today can hardly remember not having them. Plastic bags hold groceries, clothes from the cleaner and garbage for the dump. When the bags get to the dump, however, they are buried or they float around as litter. They don't biodegrade, or break down. Instead, some substances that the bags contain seep into the soil. As a result, the bags are slowly poisoning the earth.

Middle

Solving the plastic bag problem is not impossible. There are solutions, and some are more effective than others. The first is *recycling*. In 1990, people in the United States began recycling plastic bags through supermarket chains. This type of recycling has increased people's awareness that recycling is wise, but it has only slightly reduced plastic-bag pollution at the dump.

A second possible solution recommends that people *refuse*. A few conscientious people have simply gotten into the habit of saying, "No thanks, I don't want a plastic bag." If people throughout the world did this, there would be no more plastic-bag pollution. However, since busy people are slow to give up conveniences, this solution is not realistic. Most people will not refuse a plastic bag if it's offered unless an equally convenient option is proposed.

A third solution is actually being tried in South Africa and Ireland. Shoppers are required to *pay* for their shopping bags, either by purchasing them separately or by being taxed for them. This solution looks promising. In Ireland, there was a 90 per cent reduction in plastic bag use within the first five months.

A fourth solution is being tried in New Guinea in the city of Mount Hagen. Remarkably, the town has declared a total ban on plastic bags. This legal move is daring, and it sets an important example.

Ending

Most cities probably won't ban plastic bags. Yet, considering this and the other solutions can be a first step in stopping at least one form of soil pollution.

PREPARE FOR A TEST

On pages 141–143 are some writing prompts that you might find on a test. Follow each prompt and use the tips provided.

Prompt 1: Write an essay describing a person that you see every day.

Tips

▲ Read the prompt carefully.

▲ Think about the person you plan to describe. What are the person's unique features, personality traits, attitudes, or actions? How does the person smile, laugh, talk, gesture, or communicate?

▲ Plan an essay that is at least three paragraphs long.

▲ Use an appropriate system of organization, such as spatial order.

▲ Make your subject clear at the beginning of the essay.

▲ Use interesting details and sensory words. Remember that you can use a graphic organizer.

▲ Use comparisons, if they strengthen the imagery.

▲ Read through your essay to make sure it creates a clear image of the person.

▲ Check your writing to correct any errors with word forms, capitalization, punctuation, or paragraphing. Also make sure you have written complete and varied sentences.

Prompt 2: Write a story about a time when you impressed someone.

Tips

▲ Read the prompt carefully.

▲ Think about the story's main events and the order in which you want to tell them. Make it clear where and when the events took place.

▲ Make sure the story is about your own experience. Use the pronouns *I*, *me*, *we*, and *us*.

▲ Decide who else, besides you, will be a character in the story.

▲ Create a clear beginning, middle, and ending. Remember that you can use a graphic organizer.

▲ Include interesting story details.

▲ Begin a new paragraph for each new idea or piece of dialogue.

▲ Think of an attention-getting title that relates to the story.

▲ Read through your story to make sure it reads easily.

▲ Check your story for correct capitalization and punctuation, effective word use, and sentence variety.

Prompt 3: Write a fictional story about a character who has an unexpected adventure.

Tips

▲ Read the prompt carefully.

▲ Think about the story's setting. Where will it be? When will it be?

▲ Decide who will be the main character and the other characters in the story.

▲ Plan the story's events. What problem or challenge will the characters face? What will the high point be? What will the resolution be?

▲ Plan a clear beginning, middle, and ending for the story. Remember that you can use a graphic organizer.

▲ Use interesting words and sentence variety.

▲ If the story includes dialogue, make sure the characters sound like real people when they are talking. Begin a new paragraph for each change of speaker.

▲ Make sure the narrative voice is consistent throughout. The narrator should either be part of the story or separate from the story, telling about what happens to others.

▲ Read through the story to make sure it has the effect that you intend.

▲ Check the story to correct any errors in capitalization, punctuation, or word use.

Prompt 4: Write an essay explaining a goal that you have and how you plan to attain it.

Tips

▲ Read the prompt carefully.

▲ Remember that the main purpose of the essay is to explain.

▲ Plan an essay that is at least three paragraphs long.

▲ Think about the main ideas, facts, examples, and reasons that you will you use to explain your goal and tell how you plan to attain it.

▲ Think of an introductory paragraph that tells what the essay is about and makes readers want to know more.

▲ Present your ideas in a logical order, using appropriate transitional words and phrases.

▲ Write a strong ending paragraph that ties up the points in your essay.

▲ Think of a title that will get your readers' attention.

▲ Read through your essay to make sure it presents a clear explanation of your goal.

▲ Check the essay to correct any errors in capitalization, punctuation, or word use.

Tips

▲ Read the prompt carefully.

▲ Think through the main points of your opinion. Plan to clearly present your opinion in the first paragraph. Remember that you can use a graphic organizer.

▲ Your argument can be based on what you know from your own experiences or from your reading.

▲ Use convincing reasons, facts, and examples to support your position. Be sure to stick to what can be proved.

▲ Mention at least one point that someone else might use to challenge your argument and present a counterargument.

▲ Use a confident tone that will encourage readers to agree with you.

▲ Write a convincing conclusion. You may want to save your strongest reason for last.

▲ Read through your essay to make sure it is clear and convincing.

▲ Check your essay to correct any errors in capitalization, punctuation, or word use and to make sure you have good sentence variety.

Prompt 6: Write a summary of the article "Your Beating Heart" on page 144.

Tips

▲ Read the prompt carefully.

▲ As you read the article on page 144, think about its main ideas.

▲ Remember that you can use a graphic organizer.

▲ At the beginning of the summary, mention the topic of the article. Then paraphrase the article's main ideas and any essential supporting details. Present the ideas in the order in which they appear in the article.

▲ Keep your summary short and simple. Plan to make it one paragraph long.

▲ Use your own words. If necessary, quote key words, facts, or details, but don't quote long passages from the article.

▲ Make sure you don't add any ideas or opinions of your own.

▲ Read through the summary to make sure it is concise and sums up the article.

▲ Check the summary to correct any errors in capitalization, punctuation, or word use.

Read this article. Then follow Prompt 6 on page 143.

Your Beating Heart

The heart is one of the most important organs in the human body. Still, many people don't understand how their heart works. The workings of the heart, however, may not be as complicated as some think.

The Workings

The heart is a pump that sends blood through a network of vessels, or tubes, throughout the body. The heart is actually a muscle that contracts, or tightens, then relaxes. With each heartbeat, the heart muscle squeezes, and the blood flows. The contractions are usually regular because they are controlled by the heart's own timer.

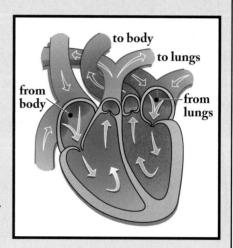

The Reasons

Why is it important that the heart beats and the blood flows? To answer this question, it helps to know how the body uses blood. Blood delivers oxygen, among other things, to the cells that make up flesh and bone. As you breathe, your lungs take in oxygen from the air. Blood passes through the lungs where it picks up the oxygen. Then the blood, now rich with oxygen, flows to the heart. The heart pumps the blood throughout the body where the cells use the oxygen they need. Then the heart pumps the "used" blood back to the lungs where it receives fresh oxygen that you have breathed. This cycle constantly repeats.

No Mixing!

It is essential that oxygen-rich blood never mixes with oxygen-poor blood. They must remain separate. For that reason, blood travels steadily in one direction through certain blood vessels and not through others. The blood vessels that carry blood away from the heart are called arteries. The blood vessels that carry blood back to the heart are called veins. The heart has another mechanism that helps keep the blood moving in one direction. One-way valves work like small flaps, or doors. They open as the heart's contractions push blood through. Between heartbeats, the valves close so that the blood cannot flow backwards.

The Parts

The heart has four main chambers, or parts. The two lower chambers are called the ventricles. The ventricles pump blood out, through the lungs, and into the rest of the body. The two upper chambers are called the atria. The atria receive blood as it is sent back from the body.

The heart, a pump with four chambers, blood vessels, valves, and a built-in clock, might be the world's most wonderful machine.

ROSEMARY WELLS

Hazel's Amazing Mother

A PUFFIN PIED PIPER

Published by
Dial Books for Young Readers
A Division of Penguin Books USA Inc.
345 Hudson Street
New York, New York 10014

The art for each picture consists of a black ink
and watercolor painting, which is color-separated
and reproduced in full color.

For Eleanor Hubbard White

Hazel's mother gave Hazel a nickel and a kiss and said, "Buy something nice for our picnic."

"I will," said Hazel, and she wheeled Eleanor's carriage down the street.

Hazel stopped to help the mailman.

"I see Eleanor has new shoes," said the mailman.

"My mother made them," said Hazel. Eleanor's shoes were sky-blue silk.

"Good morning!" said the policeman. "I see Eleanor has
a new dress."

"My mother made it," said Hazel. Eleanor's dress was
calico with French lace trim.

"Such a pretty doll," said the baker.
"My mother made her," said Hazel.
The baker gave Hazel a buttercream rose.

Hazel bought two cookies from the baker, one for herself
and one for Eleanor, but since Eleanor couldn't open
her mouth, Hazel ate them both.

With her last three pennies she bought some grapes from
the fruit lady and a piece of toast with jam from the jelly man.

"Can you find your way home, little girl?" asked the
fruit lady.

"Oh, yes," answered Hazel.

But at the next corner Hazel made a wrong turn.

After that she took another wrong turn and another,

until she found herself on a lonely hilltop in a part
of town where she had never been before.

"Don't worry, Eleanor," said Hazel. "We'll find our
way back."

Just then a boy's voice rang out, "Hey, Doris!
Someone's stealing our ball!"

In a flash Hazel was surrounded.

"What should we do, Doris?" asked the other boy.

"If she's going to play with our ball," said Doris,

"we'll play with her doll."

Eleanor was tossed from hand to hand. Off came her
blue silk shoes.

"Stop!" Hazel shouted.

Higher and farther they threw her. Off came her calico dress.
Out came her stuffing.

"No!" pleaded Hazel. But she was powerless to stop them.

When they had finished with her, Eleanor was little more than a rag.

"Eleanor, my Eleanor," said Hazel.

"Let's ride the carriage down the hill," said Doris.

Hazel rocked poor ruined Eleanor in her arms. She heard
the carriage splash into the pond at the bottom of the hill.
"Oh, Mother," she cried, "Mother, I need you!"

At just that moment, on the other side of town, Hazel's mother was picking the tomatoes for their picnic. Something told her Hazel needed her. A drop of rain fell. Then it began to pour and a great wind sprang up.

It blew the picnic blanket over the garden wall.
Hazel's mother caught hold of it but the wind was so strong

that it swept the blanket, Hazel's mother, the picnic basket, and a dozen tomatoes over the treetops as if they were no heavier than the blowing leaves.

The blanket filled with air, ballooned out, and sailed
over the town.

At last it lodged in the very tree where Hazel was sheltered
from the rain. Doris and the boys were about to run home
when Hazel's mother's voice boomed out from overhead,
"Wait just a minute!"

A tomato hit Doris smack between the eyes.

"Don't make a move without fixing Eleanor!" Hazel's mother roared.

"Who are you?" Doris squealed.

"It's my mother!" said Hazel.

"Find Eleanor's dress and shoes!" rumbled Hazel's mother.
"Restuff her and sew her up as good as new!"
Hazel's mother tossed her pocket sewing kit down to Doris.
It was followed by three more tomatoes.

The boys quivered like Jell-O. "It was all Doris's fault," they yelled.

Hazel's mother laughed thunderously. "Fish that carriage out of the pond and clean it up," she told them.

The boys scrubbed feverishly.
Doris sewed like a machine.
Above them the sun came out and the clouds slipped away.

Eleanor's carriage worked without a squeak.

Eleanor was perfect except for her eyes, which Doris could
not find in the grass.

The moment Doris and the boys left, Hazel's mother dropped
to the ground.

Hazel's mother found the eyes and sewed them back on while Hazel ate a sandwich.

"Oh, Mother," said Hazel, "how did you do it?"
"It must have been the power of love," said Hazel's mother.

Then they packed up and went home.

Hazel took two ladyfingers, one for herself and one
for Eleanor, but since Eleanor couldn't open her mouth,
Hazel ate them both.